THE MODERN SHEPHERD

The Modern Shepherd

Leadership Lessons from the Desert

AlBaraa H. Taibah

CONSTABLE

CONSTABLE

First published in Great Britain in 2019 by Constable

1 3 5 7 9 10 8 6 4 2

A CIP catalogue record for this book
is available from the British Library.

ISBN: 978-1-47213-122-5

Typeset in Sabon by SX Composing DTP, Rayleigh Essex
Printed and bound in Great Britain by Clays Ltd, Elcograf S.p.A.

Papers used by Constable are from well-managed forests
and other responsible sources.

Constable
An imprint of
Little, Brown Book Group
Carmelite House
50 Victoria Embankment
London EC4Y 0DZ

An Hachette UK Company
www.hachette.co.uk

www.littlebrown.co.uk

Shepherding teaches you patience, wisdom and caring, and connects your soul with all that is happening around you. That's what I read in books on the lessons of shepherding. That seemed odd, but I wanted to find out for myself. I wanted to know more, feel more, and live as if I'd enrolled in the school of life. Ten days in the desert, alone with a flock of sheep: I did not want to become a shepherd. I just wanted to learn how shepherding teaches you leadership.

I dedicate this book:

To my mom, who waited patiently, knowing the dangers of living alone in the desert. It was harder for her than it was for me.

To students of life. Keep observing and learning. No teacher is better than your own failures. Fail, learn, and keep moving forward.

To schools with struggling students around the world. In 2015, I visited a school in Nairobi where I saw kids hungry to learn although they had no resources. They were learning only to survive. They inspired me to go back and renovate the school fully with a computer lab, library, tablets for every class, academic plans, teacher training, sport facilities, games and much more. Education has been the focus and passion of my professional career for almost twelve years now. As a believer in education, I am donating 25 per cent of the profits from this book to organisations that support the wellbeing and skills of students in rural areas and countries. Read, learn, enjoy, and support a school.

Contents

1

Hunger for a new journey

My greatest challenge has been to change the mindset of people. Mindsets play strange tricks on us. We see things the way our minds have instructed our eyes to see.

Muhammad Yunus

It is dark, and I am being driven into the middle of nowhere with people I haven't met before. I trust them because I have no other choice, and I'm acting like there is nothing wrong with me, swallowing my fears and putting a smile onto my face. It is a fifteen-minute ride once we reach the

1

desert. I saw a grocery store where we started going off-road. To my naive mind, I thought I could use this as a landmark if I got lost. Then there were hills and valleys of sand, and we seemed to be going east and west to go north. It's only five minutes since I saw the grocery store, but I've already lost track. I know that I'll never find my landmark again. The headlights reveal the terrain a few metres ahead, but the light is sometimes blocked off by undulations. Later, I will learn that what looks like a plain landscape of sand is full of hidden signs and roads.

We reach where I will be staying, and I am invited to sit on a carpet of sand, which looks like it has been decorated with ancient Turkish designs. Soon, I am brought a cup of tea, and Abu Bandar is sitting across from me. (*Abu* means 'father' in Arabic, so Abu Bandar, which means 'father of Bandar', is the man's nickname.) With his scraggly white beard, excellent posture and heavyset frame, he looks like he has popped out of the ancient Holy Scriptures. The silence is overbearing. I have a feeling we don't speak the same language, even though Arabic is our mother tongue. He is a sixty-five-year-old Bedouin and weighs about 120 kilograms. His brown skin hints at many stories of the desert and hardship.

He is a man of the desert who uses words sparingly and doesn't respond to weak attempts to start a conversation. I ask him now, 'So what advice do you have for me, Abu Bandar?'

He pauses. The longer he does so, the more frightened I am of what he is about to say. I was taught to ask for advice, especially when faced with new challenges. As he pauses in silence, I wonder what advice he is about to give me. Surely he will tell me what I should do, how I will eat, what the weather will be like. I will learn a great deal from Abu Bandar.

Then he says, 'Beware of death.' This takes me by surprise.

He points at the desert-snake tracks in the sand embroidering the landscape around what will be my bed, the enclosure and down the slopes. 'The snake, if it bites you, you die instantly,' he tells me.

The snakes here in the Nufuth Desert – part of the Sahara – are the deadliest living creatures in existence. Grey, almost colourless, as long as an arm and thin as a finger. If they strike their victims just once, death is immediate.

I look around and all I see is black. I look at the sand, and I cannot see a thing. How will

3

I see these snakes at night? I had plans to walk barefoot. Cancelled. As I am swallowing my fear, Abu Bandar speaks again.

'Beware of thirst.' Short sentences are not helping me here. Then he continues, 'If you get lost, you will die from thirst, and we will not find you.'

So, this is my first night, and the advice I have been given is to beware death, with the assurance that if I get lost or bitten by a snake, no one will help me.

I did not want Abu Bandar to say anything else.

I want to be alone. I want to have an authentic shepherding experience, and I want to learn lessons of leadership from it, but I don't want to hear about all the other ways I could die out here in the desert.

Jeddah, Saudi Arabia, a few years earlier

It was 2004, and I was in my first year training to be an architect. Architecture amazes me and I wanted to have the skills to create out of nothing a piece of art that engages people. I did not like the sketching and drafting part of it, but I wanted to design concepts and experiences. I had started the course with high hopes for myself. But one day I was sitting in silence in an open space at the college, watching students come and go, and I was thinking less of myself. I had studied hard for an exam, but it hadn't gone well. The discrepancy between the hard work I had put in and the result put a mountain of pressure on me. The thought kept on hitting me: I have no goal in life, I am almost twenty and have achieved nothing so far, and I am certainly not making any difference. So, at that moment in the open area at the Environmental Design School at King Fahad University of Petroleum and Minerals in Saudi, I decided to change.

But what to? I was clueless and lost. I participated in every workshop, seminar and training session, and took every opportunity to learn that I could. The aim was to explore what I wanted to do. I began working part-time at the university, started a business, established a national non-profit organisation, ran the student union and supported the opening of a chapter of an international organisation in Saudi. At that time, architecture was deprioritised. I would finish my course work and try to find my sense of self-worth in all the other cool stuff I was engaged in.

All this, along with the support of friends and mentors, made me appreciate the value of learning from experience. I was learning much more outside classes than within them. This is not to minimise the value of formal education, but it is the things that I have learned in real life that have stayed with me. Lectures that I could not reflect in practice no longer exist in my memory.

Time management was one of the main lessons I learned during my bachelor's degree. I was able to run several projects at the same time, while doing a great job in most – although this is not a practice I would recommend for the long term. Upon graduation, I decided to write a book targeted at fifteen- to twenty-five-year-olds, to pass on my experiences and the things I had learned. After all the support I received from mentors and friends, I wanted to give back, and that is a value I still live by.

You Cannot Manage Time, published in 2009, was about management of oneself, not time. As time is constant and fixed, we need to adapt and utilise the time we have.

On the night of the book launch, I went back to the desk in my room and asked myself a question: What is next? What is my next project? Is it a book? I had learned from my grandfather, may he rest in peace, that I should always look forward to the next step and never stop, to take on other responsibilities so that I could add value to society.

You Cannot Manage Time was all about leading oneself, but now I was looking for a project that would help me find new ways to learn about leading others. My interest in leadership grew from my experiences at college. The self-development section was one of my favourite spots in the library, followed by the business section. As I was reading both Arabic and English books, I remembered a statement from Islamic scripture, which is a well-known phrase: 'There is no prophet who has not tended sheep.' That statement intrigued me and percolated in my head for a long time. I wanted to know why. Why was shepherding the starting point for great leaders such as Mohammed, Moses, Jesus and Abraham? How does shepherding awaken your wisdom? Empower your leadership skills? Build your character? There must be a reason and lessons to take away.

I started reading about this phrase. I wanted to know what prophets would gain from such an experience. 'It raises peace, humiliation, and patience in the shepherd,' says Dr Mebyad in

The Calling of Souls. 'Patience?' I asked myself. 'Is this because of the heat? Or because of the sheep?' Shepherding gives you 'time to meditate to understand the universe', Dr Mebyad continued. Self-reflection, humility, emotional intelligence, grit and tens of other values and traits, it turned out, were all outcomes of shepherding! But I kept questioning, 'How on earth can a flock of sheep teach you patience or humility?'

I turned to the Bible and read in John 10:11, 'I am the good shepherd; the good shepherd lays down his life for the sheep.' Then it continues in 14 with 'I am the good shepherd. I know my sheep and my sheep know me.' The depth of understanding the sheep, and the connection of mutual understanding and knowing, inspired me. Then I read in Matthew 9:36: 'When he saw the crowds, he had compassion for them, because they were harassed and helpless, like sheep without a shepherd.'

During road trips in Saudi, passing through hundreds of kilometres of sand, I had seen shepherds walking with their flocks, but while reading about the depth of that profession, I was getting excited to discover more. I was planning to start my master's degree in business administration the following year, but I also wanted to have a practical understanding of leadership.

My shepherding experience would prove to be the pivot point in my leadership practices. The contrast in my behaviour prior to shepherding and post-shepherding was astonishing. It would give me a completely different perspective on leadership.

Somewhere in the Nufuth Desert, 2011: First Night

At least I am wearing a thobe – a traditional long, white tunic with long sleeves. It was the only way I could tone down the unorthodox nature of this whole mission. The funny thing is, I had my thobe ironed because when you meet a family that lives close to the desert, it is best to look proper, even if your thobe will wrinkle the moment you sit down on the floor to have lunch or run around outside with camels. That is what I am about to learn.

I have no experience of the desert. I look nothing like a Bedouin, nothing like a Saudi, nothing like an Arab in the traditional sense, and certainly nothing like a shepherd. I look like a fresh, blond non-Arab who has just arrived from Boston, Massachusetts, where he is studying English at Kaplan. The truth is, I am Saudi, and I am on my way to experience shepherding for the first time in my life.

I was not sure what to expect. Before heading to the desert, I tried to equip myself: reading about the shepherding experience and how to adapt to the burning heat, asking people what to expect, and surely adjusting my mind to what I will face there.

Heat in the day and cold at night, that's what I learned in the geography lesson in school. At least that was a sliver of knowledge that would be useful. I packed sweaters and shorts. There is no electricity there, so I packed my flashlight. I would take my audio recorder with me and a notepad. I took a knife, yes. To be honest, none of my friends explained exactly why I would need one, but I guess watching too many movies did raise an expectation that a wolf would attack me at night. Yes, definitely a knife.

Now, here in the desert, I hear Abu Bandar's advice. I think I know why he says 'and we will not find you'. Trying to prepare as much as possible for this trip was important, and to me that meant reading, asking the advice of friends, the knife, and my summer and winter clothes. Yet, Abu Bandar has just prepared me in a deeper sense. 'We will not find you' is a mindset. He has changed my expectations. He has made me understand that the safety net has been removed: no one else can help me now, even in death. It is up to me.

At every annual Apple symposium, Steve Jobs would stand there and present Apple's new product. At the end, he would use his famous line 'and one more thing', and talk about something that takes the product beyond expectations. When you do your work as required, it is what is expected of you, but when you go the extra mile, you reach the wow factor. When teachers have high expectations of their students, students will perform better. When we buy a gift for our partner to celebrate our anniversary, it is expected, but if we miss it just once, we might end up in the desert too. When D students get a B, everyone celebrates. Yet, when an A student gets the same B, people behave with remorse. Expectations gear our minds to behave and react in ways we cannot explain rationally.

It is the same in business: if you have higher expectations of employees, productivity automatically goes up. This phenomenon is called the 'Pygmalion Effect'. Also, the reverse is true, and it is called the 'Golem Effect'.

Expectations drive our behaviours and reactions, and simultaneously our behaviours and actions define others' expectations of us. We are bound by expectations, and when needed we have to clarify our expectations. Our expectation of others will affect their behaviour too.

On my way to the desert, Abu Bandar and his sons invited me for lunch, which we ate just an hour or two ago. I did not complain about sitting on the floor, not even inwardly. We used to sit on the floor for dinner when I was a kid in my grandfather's house, until someone intervened and said we might as well use the fancy dining room because that was what it was there for. Meal sharing has evolved in Saudi Arabia. It started as one big plate of food to be shared by all on the floor, gradually transforming into a big-plate/small-plate setup, and finally graduating into the meal-table setup, with several plates of food and an individual plate for everyone. People's hands no longer touch in the middle like they used to. Families were closer to one another when they shared a single plate of food, and the dining table has created a divide. So I found it good to experience this old-fashioned setup again with Bandar's family.

I met Abu Bandar through a friend of mine who I had got to know in the USA. My friend's relative, Bandar, is the eldest son of Abu Bandar. It's strange that I picked up Abu Bandar's trail on a continent that is the farthest thing possible from his identity. I doubt there are nomadic shepherds in America who speak a rough version of Arabic.

After lunch, I looked to my left at Abu Bandar, who was driving. We were on our way to the middle of the desert, where I knew his large herd of sheep was waiting for my wise and tender shepherding. Waiting for me to know exactly what to do. Waiting for me to lead them from home and back. I told myself that this shouldn't be difficult. But as we left all signs of civilisation, I realised that my heart was sinking down between my feet. There was nothing but desert all around, and the sun was hotter than a blazing grill.

Here's what I knew about sheep: they make for good meals at Eid, the holiday after the holy pilgrimage, the Hajj, is over. I was also pretty sure I knew how to imitate their bleating when I was a child learning animal sounds. So what I really knew about sheep was nothing. Reading about shepherding in books doesn't count.

Anxiety settled in firmly during that drive. Anxiety is a malady that is hard to shake off, especially when we fear for our own safety. Ten days alone in the middle of the desert could be the death of me. It really could. There is no exaggeration there. Nevertheless, there I was handing my life over to the elements, to this man who was driving me, to this car that was speeding ever forward into sand and oblivion. And into nature, which always presents us with wonders and surprises.

When I scoured dozens of books before this crazy adventure, I came across vague descriptions of the harshness of nature . . . the desert where many get lost and forgotten, the heat that dries all liquid, the animals that are so fragile they sometimes survive only for a day. But the truth is, I did not honestly think about what I was getting into until that moment. Now I realise why: I did not want to hold myself back from going. If I'd thought about the dangers too much, I would have grown too scared to attempt the adventure. After all, I would essentially be alone for ten days, and even if I screamed for help, there would be no one to hear me. The closest neighbourhood would be miles of waterless sand in any direction. And I had no idea where that grocery store was!

Trees are sparse here. On the journey, I was surprised by the sight of one or two, but the distance between them was like the distance between myself and Abu Bandar. The terrain became smoother, which to the eye was pleasing but to the mind a sign of danger. It only meant that the desert was getting more real. The desert seduces you with silk and curves but offers nothing for your survival.

I tried to think of some way to start a conversation with this man to ease my nerves, but every line of thought melted like ice cream in the heat before I got the chance to form the words. There was nothing I could possibly say to him to sustain a conversation.

Still, I tried: 'It's so hot.'

He snorted and kept his eyes on the road. Of course it's hot. It's the deadliest height of summer.

I left my apartment in Cambridge, Massachusetts, only three days ago. It was green there. The flowers and wild things were in bloom, and lemonade stands stood on every street corner. If you were to walk through the fens, on the other side of the Charles River, you would have found yourself walking into lush, unruly landscapes and little gardens, side by side, each tended by a Bostonian who doesn't have a backyard. It's so pleasant and charming in Boston – it's a wonder I was able to release myself from its spell and bring myself over to this side of the planet where the summer is merciless. I arrived in Riyadh, Saudi Arabia, just yesterday, telling no one in my family what I planned to do until last night. I myself tried not to think about it.

'I'm going away for ten days,' I told my grandmother.

'Where are you going?'

How to say this?

'I'm going to the desert. To tend a flock of sheep.'

It was challenge to assure her that I would be safe because I didn't know what to expect myself. She thought I was crazy and started praying for me. I started praying for me, too.

I looked at my reflection in the wing mirror. My skin would definitely burn like a lobster. I have what they call 'coloured eyes'. My blue-green pigmentation would surely allow more light into my retina, but I didn't allow myself the luxury of sunglasses. Just like ancient times, I told myself as I packed. This is not an experiment in comfort, nor is it an experiment in modernity.

■ ■ ■

'You'll see it in a minute,' said Abu Bandar.

So, I thought, he *does* speak.

We had been in the car for half an hour. Fifteen minutes driving to a town called Zulfi, which is a godforsaken spot I had never heard of, and then fifteen minutes in the desert, off-road. Driving through this sand had killed any hope I had of escaping even if I wanted to. With all the terrains and sand dunes, I couldn't even remember which direction Zulfi was in.

There is no way to tell direction here, except for a strong memory of the route, which only Abu Bandar has. He sees these seemingly identical pieces of terrain as landmarks different in shape, with an invisible coordinate on top of them identifying the location.

I could feel my stomach slipping lower and lower as we delved into the oblivion of sand. What am I getting myself into? Why didn't I just take a leadership course back in Boston? Why didn't I watch the documentary about shepherds? There *must* have been a documentary about shepherds.

While my family would have approved my taking a nice, quiet, safe course about leadership, I had decided to study leadership in the rigorous school of life. But I might have underestimated how hot the classroom would be.

When the enclosure came into view, Abu Bandar stopped the car and told me to hop out.

'Woah!' I exclaimed. It was above 50°C, around 120 °F. The sun was already boring a hole through my head.

And so now I am here. Tea with Abu Bandar, a warning about my possible demise, and a chance to get my bearings.

Six male sheep and 105 female sheep are surrounded in an enclosure by a wooden fence. There's a small storage shack for keeping hay bales, and – for sleeping – two raised wooden boards beneath a canopy of palm shavings. I see a well and endless dunes all around. They're like expanses of earth that have not been formed yet into any useful or solid shape. The edge of the game board, the void in the grid, and I am the avatar that strayed outside the playing area.

Before I came, I was told by everyone I shared my mission with that I was not cut out for this. They told me I would not last, that I would not be able to handle it. To be lost in this desert is as deadly as the bite of the snake, Abu Bandar is saying. If you don't find your way back in time, dehydration will kill you, he explains. You will not last a day without water. My mind is full of challenging messages and demotivational vibes. So venom and dehydration are very possible in the next few days. Nice. No problem. At this point I just want to complete my mission alive. Screw leadership.

A man named Abram appears from inside the shed. He is a young Nepali nearing his thirties with a face that looks more Far Eastern than anything else. He has skin that has been braised and broiled in the sun. He wears a simple, threadbare, throw-on thobe with no cuffs, collars or seams. I feel very fancy in my own thobe. Abram, who works for Abu Bandar, is the true shepherd around here. He is the man who will be teaching me the ropes. He is the man the sheep follow and trust.

Also, he does not speak English or Arabic. Great. So how am I going to learn anything from him?

As the night is coming to an end Abu Bandar leaves me to commence my journey to becoming a shepherd. I walk towards my 'bedroom', 50 metres away. The two wooden benches, one for me and another for Abram, are raised a metre above ground. I look up, I can see the sky from my own bed. I look around, and there are no walls. My bed is in the middle of nowhere with nothing around it. I come to realise that the board is raised so the snakes cannot reach it. How comforting.

I lie down on my bed, with absolute silence around, thinking about the books I read and the friends to whom I talked to help me prepare for this experience. I think of my friends' many words of concern and Abu Bandar's few words of warning. I am frightened, and it is only the first night.

2

A determined shepherd

Life is the best teacher, just as it is. It is the toughest teacher. It won't tolerate slothfulness for long. It's always throwing some difficult problem your way and then seeing what you will do with it.

Stephanee Killen

Nufuth Desert, 2011: Day One

I don't know how darkness came so fast. My first day has just raced by. I've been caught up with fears in my head, trying to plan out some kind of solid strategy to stay alive for the next ten days. All the plans somehow melt into each other because they are only the disguises of fear. Instead of showing itself for what it is, fear plans and devises all sorts of survival schemes. I forget all of the plans when night falls. I realise there is no plan. There is only sheer terror, and it is mounting. I have nothing else to do but feel the blackness of it for hours on end. I can't help but reflect on how I foolishly thought this would be easy.

It is not only the dark that frightens me, but the fact I can't ask for help when needed or run back to the city, especially as I am lying above writhing snakes waiting for me to leave my bed and be their goodnight supper. I am missing home. When there is an emergency at night, we pick up the phone and call 911. When we have a nightmare, we turn on the light, and when we are thirsty, we can simply turn on the tap to drink water. Now that basic necessities have been taken away from me and I can no longer choose what to do, I treasure the luxury of having options.

There is no source of light here but the moon. A flat blackness with no city lights, not even distant pinpricks on the highway. I shudder to think that I could have accidentally chosen to be here when there would be no moon. I look up at the moon and send a wave of gratitude.

I am no longer oozing with sweat. With the sun gone, I can feel myself relaxing. But I don't leave the wooden bed. Not tonight. I will not be poisoned to death, at least not on the first night. I sit cross-legged, and suddenly wish my thobe was threadbare and thin. I wish I hadn't starched it. Everything around me is flowing, and there seems to be as much potential for chaos as there is for orderly solitude.

Abu Bandar left me with Abram. The young man, I quickly learned, is a sheep whisperer. Well, he never talks to them, but he understands both the obvious and subtle needs of every animal in the herd. I watched him all day today because there was nothing for me to do.

Abram could be featured in *National Geographic* as one of those human beings who lives in an untouched community somewhere in a desolate valley to which no one has ever travelled. I learned from Abu Bandar that Abram has not taken a vacation in three years. If I were to tell you that you were going to spend a week in Hawaii, you would feel excited, wouldn't you? Abram would feel the same way if you gifted him a prepaid card from the telecom company so he could call his family in Nepal.

This is what I learned from Abram the first day: shepherding is the most boring and yet exhausting job. You would think that all you had to do was take the livestock to where they feed and bring them back again, making sure no predators come close. But there is more to it than that, and nothing about it is fun. The more sheep there are, the harder the job. Abram can't take a vacation, call in sick or decide that his lunch break is more important than theirs. Abram is here for them. Every single sheep matters here.

I continue to appreciate the options we have in our lives. The option to skip a meeting, to switch on a light, to sleep a few minutes more, to call in sick, to walk barefoot at night. When all options bar the way of the desert are removed, you are guided towards one path only. Will Smith once said, when explaining the reason for his success, 'If we are racing on a treadmill together, I either win, or I die.' Not having other options is the first insight that has been forced upon me by the desert. It is fundamentally different to playing to win. It is playing to survive.

When we try to stop a bad habit, it's the option to quit trying that makes it difficult. Or when we are on a diet and we don't commit, it's because we have the option to eat the cake or the big fat delicious burger. The desert changes your mindset with a reality check: you have no options. Your mind adjusts to a state of being where you realise you only have one way ahead and no option but to make it happen. I am a committed person, but this is different. I have no choice but to commit: the only way is the desert way.

Grit and not giving up indicate that we have other options to choose from, but we are absolutely committed to one. Many successful leaders of all types – Henry Ford, Oprah Winfrey, Walt Disney, Steve Jobs – have mastered changing their mindsets to one of not giving up; they put their minds into a state where is no option: 'I either win, or I die.' And if failure nevertheless does happen, it is only an opportunity to try again, with more experience behind you. Grit, or will, is described as one of the key elements shared by Level 5 leaders in *Good to Great: Why Some Companies Make the Leap . . . and Others Don't* by Jim Collins. He explains that Level 5 Leadership is almost about 'stoic determination to do whatever needs to be done to make the company great'.

The mind is a powerful tool, which can be used to remove the acceptance of other options.

It is difficult to have that mindset, grit and strong will in everything you do, in both your personal and professional life. It can foster professional competency, but it can also aid our health, for example. I always have many options that mean that I don't have to commit to that diet or gym class, but the difference is all in my mind. At a young age, we have the freedom to deprioritise health, wrongly so, but at an older age, if we want to live, we have no option but to prioritise our health. The only way is the healthy way.

In the desert, if you want to keep your flock alive, there is no option but to shepherd. The sheep need to be fed at the crack of dawn, around 6 a.m. Their water tanks need to be filled because, whether they slurped up all the water or not the preceding day, the heat of the sun will have finished the job by evening. The sheep eat and drink for about two hours, and that is the time when Abram tends to them. He checks for illness, milks the females, looks over the young and cleans their eyes. Little insects can swarm around sheep's eyes and drive them mad. Once these rituals are complete, the sheep are led to their arid and hopeless pasture where only dry sprigs shoot up from the ground, and how those serve their bodies, I cannot imagine.

I'm no botanist, but those plants look like they have barely enough nutrients to stay alive.

Shepherds must keep their sheep safe from wolves and snakes. Like a human, a sheep will fall dead instantly if bitten by a snake. Luckily, I've been assured there are no wolves in this area. Thank God for that, because I have no idea what sort of martial arts I would have to pull off in front of a wolf.

The sheep head back to their pen once they are sated, practically with no need to be rounded up. They do this because they are trained. Abu Bandar said to me, 'If the sheep were trained to pray, they would pray.'

So this is the way it is. They know what they're about, those sheep. They know their way around. They are my guides instead of me being theirs.

Abram probably thinks I'm crazy for sitting around and watching him all day. But this is how I learn. Demonstration is the only mode of communication between us so far. It is illuminating to spend hours alone with another human being with whom I cannot speak. The absence of words brings forward the humanity that we both share so keenly, and I feel gratitude rushing in, in large doses. This simple man does these tedious tasks every single day in this desolation, so far away from his family. He does not have the vast inventory of luxuries of my own cosmopolitan life, but perhaps he is also free of some of the unyielding complications that don't serve me at all. I think about the arguments, the many decisions, the emotional and practical gripes we constantly create for ourselves.

I have to drink two gallons of water from the well and keep my skin moistened to soothe the heat. A plastic gallon bottle would melt in the heat, so you sink a canvas bag in water, then wrap the bottle with it, and the wet bag does a cooling job as well as any refrigerator. I learn how to make my own natural air conditioner by sprinkling water around me on the ground where I sit during the day. I cover my tender scalp with a piece of cloth that I shape into a makeshift turban to keep my head from burning under the sun.

When you're out in the open desert, the combination of heat and physical exertion can be merciless. Try walking for hours on soft sand. You will soon forget about your StairMaster. You grow muscles from walking on the sand and up the hills. The closer the contours on the sand, the firmer and more comfortable the ground is to walk on. Soft sand will hold your feet, and gymnastic skill is required to pull them out and keep on walking for miles.

Against the backdrop of the desert's silence, the challenges and hardship threw me back to a construction site in Saudi Arabia, 2010.

It was eleven o'clock in the morning and I was overseeing the site. The building was to be completed for handover that day by 4 p.m. It had been renovated from the foundations to the rooftop, but we had just discovered a crucial mistake.

I was working for Turner Construction, one of the world's leading construction companies, which had been established in the USA in 1904 and has a branch in the Middle East called Turner Arabia. We had been given the job of completing some buildings at King Abdullah University for Science and Technology – KAUST. The university's campus, which is akin to a city in its own right and was one of the king's largest projects, was still being completed. KAUST was the king's baby.

As our deadline was approaching quickly, Saudi Aramco, the client representative, doubled its effort to help us finish the job. I didn't have a huge amount of experience, but had been promoted by my mentor, Majid AlArgoubi, to be the one in charge.

I was still fresh out of King Fahad University of Petroleum and Minerals, proud of my architectural engineering degree, and had started on the lowest rung on the ladder only a year earlier. I was the guy who took pictures of the construction site and managed the tracking sheet. I smiled my way up the rungs very quickly, and I learned the benefits of praising others and of being dependable. Majid, a project leader on site at the Aramco–KAUST Project Management Office, began to see that I am the kind of guy who respects the clock, respects the team, and can get the workers going like I'm chasing them with dynamite.

He had given me my first building, one out of the total of sixty-four buildings that the whole project comprised. I needed to make sure the foundations were sound, the walls were painted, the electricity was wired correctly, and so forth. The building had to be squeaky clean and ready to be inspected so that we could officially hand it over to become KAUST property.

I always met my deadlines early. Majid was impressed by my speed, so he handed me more buildings until I had eleven new projects to deliver, including the one I was due to hand over that day. I was on fire, along with four engineers and around six hundred skilled and non-skilled labourers.

That day, however, at precisely five past eleven in the morning, Majid called and gave me grave news. Four walls in the building were missing concrete blocks.

The way it usually happens is that gypsum board walls have solid concrete blocks sandwiched between them during the foundational phase of construction. I knew that the process of taking down the walls, stacking and cementing the concrete, putting the walls back up, smoothing the putty over the walls and letting it dry, then repainting the walls and allowing them to dry again – all of that would take two days *minimum* to achieve.

I remembered that life is full of choices, and that the decisions we make forge a unique path forward for every one of us. I had to make a choice between allowing the process to take its normal time and pushing the deadline, if I could manage it, or taking a supernatural risk by trying to complete the task before the 4 p.m. deadline, when KAUST's top management were coming to sign off on the building's completion and Aramco would no longer be responsible for it. That morning, I chose in favour of risk, in the hope of proving my dependability: to eliminate all other choices and focus on delivery. 'We will sign off that building,' I assured myself.

I gathered all my willpower to create a strategy during the lunch break, then contacted the best men in the team.

I carefully selected four workers for each phase of the process: building the concrete, cutting out the gypsum board, applying the putty and painting. I had come up with an outlandish plan to beat the clock. While four workers built the concrete foundations, I had four others cut out the gypsum board and lay it on the floor. Then four other workers applied the putty and dried it as fast as they could with the help of a host of fans I had brought into the building. We painted the gypsum board while the concrete builders were finishing their work, and by the time the concrete was set, the walls were ready to be put up. We used putty to smooth the seams as we set the walls onto their foundations, so that would be the only thing that was still wet by the time the client came in.

I ran around the construction site, feeling like a choreographer with heart palpitations. I was sweating right through my clothes.

We finished before the deadline, at 3.15 p.m. Majid did not believe me when I called and told him the problem was already fixed.

As the desert pushes me towards one only option, I feel the similarities between this and being pushed by KAUST to finish and hand over the building. I have no option but to complete what I have started. I am respecting Abram more and more.

As for the sheep . . . well, they run from me. They treat me as if I am an annoying gust of wind that keeps blowing at them. They know their way to and from the pasture without my help. When I come towards them from the right, they run to the left. When I come from the left, they go to the right. I am desperate to prove myself as a good guide. It is not until later that I understand that the sheep and I have different agendas.

Whenever I approach to guide them towards the pasture, they think I'm chasing them and take off. So I let them go to the pasture on their own, and I walk slowly behind them, matching their pace whenever they start running. I can almost hear them saying, 'Who is that chasing us?'

Reality strikes me: have I just been rejected by a flock of sheep? I came to them as their new shepherd. If only I could introduce myself in a way that would make them understand and accept me. But how can I communicate what's happening? And should the message be that I am here to lead, to support, or to learn from them? I am certainly not Abram, nor do I speak sheep. Abu Bandar told me that originally a shepherd would go with the sheep to the pasture while sitting on a donkey. He said that sheep usually follow a donkey. The shepherd, when he had found the perfect spot for the herd to graze, would tie the donkey to a tree. Where the donkey would sit, the sheep would gather, and that is how they would know where their perimeters were.

Well, I'm barely recognised in the sheep community, and I don't have a donkey. So I ask myself: what am I going to do? I don't feel like much of a shepherd.

This is the perfect time to quit. Well, for one, Abu Bandar is expecting that from me, so there is no failure there. Death is just around the corner, or under the bed in this case, the flock is running away from me, and I don't speak sheep. I think it's time to sleep.

I am very tired, and it is only day one.

3

Discovering a new me, deep in the desert

I remind myself every morning: Nothing I say this day will teach me anything. So if I'm going to learn, I must do it by listening.

Larry King

The Nufuth Desert, 2011: Day Two

I wake up at dawn. The stillness here is so incredibly peaceful that you feel like you are born again when the sun starts to come up. I look over at the pen. The sheep are beginning to move.

I get up with new resolve. Maybe the sheep need to know their shepherd before he can shepherd them. After all, they have not appointed me as their shepherd, nor can Abram introduce me to them, or can he? If the sheep were humans, I would have introduced myself and flashed them a smile. I would have taken the time to get to know each one of them. Some would have been open with me and others would have been reserved, which would have been all right. But these sheep are not humans. So I figure food is the key. That's a language all living beings understand, right? So before Abram arrives, I set out their food for them myself and fill up the water tanks. I hope this works.

I come from a school of thinking that places people as the most important asset in any organisation: take care of your people, and they will take care of the business. Yet, connecting with your colleagues is not as easy as it sounds, it requires an investment of both effort and time. Connecting to your colleagues continues to be dragged down the list of priorities, like a drowning man in the pool trying to reach the surface to breathe. Achieving targets always wins the battle and claims its position at the top of the list of priorities.

The sheep still run from me to the other side of the pen.

'That's all right,' I say to them, 'you can run if you like, but it'll be me feeding you from now on.' Their eyes are on me as I set out their food.

I am claiming responsibility and accountability for the flock. I will connect with them. Leaders are accountable for the wellbeing of their team, as well as financial and business targets. Majid taught me a great deal about that, and my experience at university also pushed me to connect with the team.

Developing connections, however, is tricky in reality. A few years after my experience in the desert, I was just completing a project and was ready to move to another job and a new challenge. I found both in the form of a national project to engage stakeholders and develop a strategy based on multi-level studies and research. There was a team of fifteen members in place when I took on my role. In the first week, I noticed a crazy deadline with a major workload. Understanding the team was crucial to me, but I prioritised targets over connecting with the team. We completed the tasks but damaged relationships. After completion, I asked the team for feedback, and not to my surprise they felt isolated, disconnected and driven to execution rather than leading the project. At the time, I realised that I had failed the leader in me and empowered the manager in me whose sole purpose was to get the job done.

The flock and I don't speak the same language; I cannot become a shepherd before I connect. Even if I offer them food on one occasion, that does not make me their shepherd.

A manager has the right to claim authority, but they will only get what is required from the team. No one will go the extra mile and challenge themselves for greater results. You can only lead if you have a personal connection. It starts from within the team, their belief in their leader and the organisational mission.

You must connect not only to other team members, but to yourself. With the sheep, I wonder if it's crazy to be talking to them. I realise as the day wears on that the silence is making my head so full of noise that I speak it out loud just to relieve the pressure. In my organised and bustling life, I had not been aware that I had so many thoughts. In this silence, they all beep like cars in rush-hour traffic.

Ideas are bumping all around my head, but this starts to be boring because it's one-way traffic.

So I start talking to myself as if I'm two people at once, and soon I find myself presenting cases to myself and arguing them, with the other me taking on the role of devil's advocate. Sometimes the other me becomes convinced by the argument. Sometimes he doesn't. Sometimes I double back and find another angle to the argument that makes him give in.

With all the time I have on my hands watching sheep eating ash disguised as plants, I find myself exploring all the points of view that exist in the universe. I discover perspectives I wasn't sure existed, then start convincing myself with arguments I normally would have opposed. I think about matters such as my master's degree, nursing, the quality of dates in Saudi Arabia, my mother's young life, my father's young life, my grandfather's young life, and even whether ballpoint pens are better than fountain pens. I also think about why I am me. What is my calling? What is my focus in life? Why is it I am with the sheep and not at the beach? How there is a voice to silence . . . a teacher in an animal . . . the diversity in the world . . . what brings people together . . . a school in the desert.

It makes my mind hurt to overwork it this way, but it seems a natural by-product of being alone in silence, like a purging process. I hope that afterwards there will be silence in my mind, too. It does not feel like the silence will be approaching anytime soon. There is just too much of a backlog in there.

The interesting thing about me splitting myself into two persons is that I'm able to split into a third and observe how arguments between people – or egos, if you will – tend to take place. Each has a valid point to offer the other, if they are able to find it, and the more I practise finding this valid point, the more I feel my own reserve and judgement of people slip away, like a silk sash off a table. I find wisdom in venting the noise out of my brain and accepting all perspectives, even those I rightfully oppose. I don't know if I can say that everyone in the world is right, but I find myself, as this process continues, accepting that everyone has a standpoint and that, from their perspective, it is valid. So where does that leave us? I don't know really. But I do appreciate the peace this gives me. I no longer feel the need to defend. I am finding a deeper meaning through connection.

Perspectives and opinions are derived from experiences and past behaviours. To change minds, we need to enrich knowledge and experience. Arguing might lead to a temporary state of approval, but the mind will settle back to where it belongs. In *Our Iceberg is Melting*, John Kotter highlights a NoNo character who is negative and finds the worst in every idea. Kotter emphasises the importance of such a character to a team: they enlighten perspectives and point out risks that enthusiasts would probably skip. We should not fear an opposition to our thoughts and beliefs, because it will either strengthen them or correct them.

In the desert, I find wisdom in the diversity of thoughts, and strengthening relationships and connections creates a safe bridge along which to transmit these thoughts. Having connected to yourself, you can connect to your team, connect to your mission, and connect to your values. Life will test our values, ethics and beliefs, and only those who are true to themselves will find truth and happiness within.

When my arguments wear themselves out, I realise I really need to talk to someone. Anyone!

Jeddah, Saudi Arabia, 2013

It's two years after my stint as a shepherd, and I'm fresh out of my master's degree programme.

The degree in Business Administration confirms that I should be able to lead an organisation, and it's time for me to confirm that by leading the oldest organisation in civilisation: a school. At twenty-nine years old, I am probably the youngest principal of a school ever in Saudi Arabia.

I'm in the meeting room with the whole faculty of DAT boys' school. I can hear the boys running and panting near the window. It's recess, and it's the perfect chance for the staff to get together and leave the children outside. I recall how hot and bothersome it felt to run outside in the heat and humidity of Jeddah, a major city in the western region, when I was a boy. I wonder if we have a budget for mist sprays to cool the boys off.

DAT is a private school that combines all three levels of schooling: elementary, middle and high school. Under its roof there are about 2000 students and 150 teachers. The school is twelve years old and it is one of the top-performing schools in the region, although it is not functioning very innovatively. This is where I come in.

I turn my attention to the room. A circle of what I perceive to be sceptics greets me at the meeting table. This will require a moment of courage, because all of the men at this table have more experience of education than I do. They are also older than I am. Much older. Some of them were my teachers when I was running around at recess.

The board has decided to hire me, I think, because they believe that the educational system is getting tired. They want to see what a young person can do for the school. It is an attempt, I believe, to air the school and allow fresh circulation into its longstanding buildings and routines.

The members of the faculty who are sitting in front of me, however, seem very comfortable with the stale old air. They have been breathing it for the past few decades, and their fragile little world seems to have held firm so far. Here comes AlBaraa with a sledgehammer. I shall convey the message of change, and share my thoughts and aspirations for this school. I am sure they will love it, and I will convince them that it works. But keeping a great idea in check in order to release it at the right time requires strength, strength I learned from the desert. I remind myself to be gentle. I shall connect first. I put the sledgehammer down.

I take my seat, heart pounding. *Courage, Baraa.* I give them my sunniest smile. I've smiled my way through life, and I intend to smile my way through this meeting.

'Good afternoon! How's everybody doing?' I start.

General assent that everyone is doing very well, thank you very much.

The faculty waits. So I launch into my prepared speech about teamwork and common goals and extending a hand to one another. I take care not to impose my agenda for educational renovation too soon. When I'm done, I humbly tell them that I am eager to hear their thoughts and that I'd be honoured to get to know them better.

The sceptics remain quiet. I can tell who they are by their narrowed eyes, dejected expressions and distance from the table. The more cooperative teachers speak up and introduce themselves with reciprocated smiles.

Reflecting what I learned in the Sahara is not easy. I feel the pressure of accountability, and it's hard to manage the mixed emotions of starting a new job in a new field. The only reaction I received from the flock of sheep was that they ran away from the newcomer; now I feel a room full of questions and suspicion.

I calm myself down, manage my emotions and commit to trying to connect. I try to learn things about my staff. I approach them like we are one big family. I ask about hobbies and favourite foods. I find out that some teachers are away from home. I ask what they do in their free time. Mr S. D. shares early on that his family is expecting a baby in May. Our meeting brings us closer, yet the teachers are still suspicious that a trap has been laid. 'We are not used to being heard,' one of them shares with me later. When everyone is done, a man I haven't noticed clears his throat.

This is M. M., an Egyptian teacher in his elder years. He unclasps his hands from over his stomach and leans forward. His voice comes out in a thick, long drawl.

'Ustaz Baraa!' he begins. *Ustaz* means teacher or mister in Arabic. *Here we go*, I think to myself.

'How old are you?' he asks.

'I am twenty-nine years old.'

And into my head comes the image of the flock running away from me as I approach.

A ripple of amusement passes around the table.

'Here is what I know, Ustaz Baraa,' he says, enunciating. 'One begins first as a teacher, and from there he is promoted to head of his level and then moves up to become principal. How is it that you who have never even taught a class became the principal of this school?'

I am not prepared for that one.

He continues explaining the question, which gives me time to prepare an answer. Then he stares, waiting to hear what I have to say.

'I'd love for us to have a talk, and I will tell you everything you wish to know about my previous experience and why I am capable of leading this school,' I reply. 'But I need your word on one thing.'

He looks at me anxiously.

'I hear you're very well liked around here. I want you to spread your faith in me, once you have it, as principal – spread faith among the other teachers in a positive future for this school. We need to join hands together.'

Ustaz M. M. raises himself a couple of inches with pride.

I walk away feeling empowered and only slightly shaken. This man pierced my confidence for a second.

A lack of confidence is the most raw feeling, and it is especially difficult to hide. I believe that once it is seen in a leader's eyes, it is very difficult for him or her to be redeemed. I could not tell if Ustaz M. M. and the rest saw me trip and fall internally, but I have hopes that now, at least, they seem to be more on my side.

4

The desert outgrows
my determination

Caring about the happiness of others, we find our own.

Plato

The Nufuth Desert, 2011: Day Three

I am a determined shepherd. The sheep still run
from me when I approach, but I adopt an air of
nonchalance. Abram typically opens the gate for
them in time for their morning spree. But today,
I decide to open the gate for them in the afternoon. I'm playing it cool with the sheep. In no

time, they will begin to recognise me. At least, I hope.

After all, what choice have they got? For the duration of this experiment, when Abram is not around there is no one else but me to sustain their lives. Shepherding these sheep is a delicate business. There is no shirking in this job, not even for an extra hour of sleep. You need to wake up in time to feed them, so that they will finish eating in time for the next thing and the next. They depend on you to protect them from dehydration. I learned that a sheep cannot survive a day without water in this heat. Just like humans.

In the pasture, you are committed to remain with them until they've had their fill and begin to turn home. You cannot leave them out in the open and run back for something. You need to be prepared to be stuck in the desert in the scorching heat until the sun gets too fierce and the sheep cannot walk on hot sand any more. Then and only then can you turn back with your herd safely under your watch.

For example, I forgot my turban today and did not realise it until I was in the pasture with them. I had to hold a branch of leaves over my head and alternate arms whenever I got tired. I had to pour water on it from my carefully measured water supply. There was no other choice.

Now we're back, and I watch Abram as he performs his magic with each and every animal, checking them for injuries or maladies after their romp in the pasture. In this desolation, I wonder if his ability to listen and feel are naturally heightened. He simply listens and feels the need of the animal. By touch, he knows the pain or tension from which the animal suffers. By the subtle sounds they make, he hears the wordless complaint. He's known the sheep since they were lambs, Abu Bandar explained to me. The unconditional care Abram shows towards every single sheep is inspiring. When you know an animal from the day it is born, you grow accustomed to its ways, habits and modes of expression.

As Abram is magically dancing between the sheep, I see love and compassion and care all around the flock. I am not a sheep whisperer like Abram, but I can see how each sheep is waiting for its turn to receive the needed care. He cleans the eye of one, milks another, checks the tongue of the others. I don't think I will ever be able to tell the difference between them, but Abram knows.

A leader would tell you to care for your people. It's a repeated phrase in every leadership book, it's something almost everyone knows, but not everyone reflects it in practice. Abram realises that our only asset is the flock, nothing else. His care for their wellbeing is inspiring, and it is even more inspiring that his care is customised to each individual sheep.

In large organisations, we start losing the sense of individuality and get accustomed to clusters and groups – we start treating people as numbers. People do not want to be treated as a number, they want to be an added value and grow together with the organisation. On the other hand, if you communicate with care, this alerts others who want to take advantage and ask for favours. Our good intentions are hurt by the acts of the few and translated into materialistic views and paybacks. Our intentions are put into question.

Individualised learning is a key concept in education and teaching: we care about the individual student. Skillsets are different from one person to another, and the beauty of team work is to capitalise on each individual's strength. An orchestrated symphony with each holding a different instrument.

As I was about to graduate from my master's in education leadership, I received the offer to become the principal of DAT school. At first, I was afraid to accept it, as I had no previous experience in schools or in education. I wanted to set my expectations and equip my mindset accordingly. I once asked my professor, Ms Ellen, who taught my education leadership classes, 'How would the school principal knows if he is doing a good job in school?' A school as an organisation has many targets: teacher performance, student outcomes, positive culture, and many more. But what Ms Ellen shared with me was that care can be practised in any organisation, leading to a deeper under-standing of the individual. 'Your teachers are humans, and they all have personal and professional issues,' she said. I was wondering how their per-sonal problems would relate to my performance as a school principal when Ms Ellen continued, 'When these issues are replaced with issues about students and their learning, you then succeed.'

From experience, I can now acknowledge that this is correct. Caring about every individual teacher diverted their fears from their personal and professional issues and allowed them to concen-trate on their students. Establishing a comfortable environment through a culture of customised care will erase all other fears and worries, so everyone can happily focus on solving business problems.

Richard Branson repeatedly emphasises and shares the ways in which he takes care of the Virgin team. He shepherds them, connects and cares about their wellbeing. Unlike many other organisations that put clients first, Branson emphasises that 'Clients do not come first. Employees come first.' It is not that clients have a lower priority – on the contrary. 'If you take care of your employees, they will take care of the clients' is a strategy for prioritising care that results in happy clients.

I look at the sheep again and find them too similar for me to spot the subtle differences between them. It's like looking at a certain ethnic group with unaccustomed eyes, unable to see past the general similarity that the people's faces display on the surface. But Abram knows every sheep. I tune in with him as he makes his rounds, but find myself rejected from this small cult of understanding.

There is nothing glamorous about shepherding. The odour of the livestock is rank and overpowering. You need to tread through a field of their faeces in order to get close to them. It takes a while for your naked nostrils to become numb to the smell. You need to learn to live with your sweat, to protect yourself in every way you can from dehydration. The routine is rigid, and the bed is hard.

I open the gate for the sheep in the afternoon, feeling a sense of accomplishment. I am here for a good reason, after all. They leave for their spree in the pasture and I follow them.

Again, I am faced with the expanse of desert that is now mimicking the expanse of thoughts I am thinking right now with no distractions. I prepare myself for another torrent of monologues, and for the monologues to split into dialogues. As hours turn into dust, I try not to worry too much about losing my mind.

I try to get nearer to the sheep. The frontal approach, of course, would fail because they would see me and run. So I try to creep up on one sheep from behind, having become rather expert at sneaking around on the sand. Before I can get to within fifteen metres, the creature hobbles off, extending its offended face and snapping its jaws. That's what I get for rushing our friendship.

Maybe that one is having a bad day. I decide to try again with another. So I sneak up behind a second sheep in the hope that it will stand still as I try to pet its back.

The creature runs from me like I'm carrying a disease. My ego is bruised.

Our relationship is still not going well. I need to find another way to connect and care.

Five years after my shepherding experience, I led a national project to set standards and license educators in Saudi. The project involved developing national standards for teachers, a licensing system and supporting elements to help gradually improve the quality of teachers in the kingdom. Even if I spent the rest of my life teaching in classrooms, my opinions and ideas could not represent all thirteen states in Saudi and over five hundred thousand teachers. The stakes were high as well: these standards would be the baseline for all professional examinations, licensing and job evaluation. Furthermore, teachers were objecting to the project and were standing in the way of its success. I was worried: how could we run a project while its major stakeholders were rejecting its existence?

I was astonished by the similarities: whether I was trying to improve a school or teacher standards, at first people would not connect with me, some would question me, and others might attack. The team and I decided to execute a strategy of engagement with care. We flipped the structure, and we positioned teachers as the authors of the standards; we engaged representatives in all thirteen states to share their thoughts, and engaged them again to confirm what they shared; and empowered them as owners of their standards.

We ran workshops, focus groups and surveys highlighting one message only: that your voice not only matters, it is needed to draft the standards. We cared. We listened to teachers with interesting insights on social media, we replied to every idea, and we showed care in making connections.

The day we launched the standards, teachers were celebrating and promoting them. The gap in behavioural change was due to us making genuine connections and implementing a strategy of care for individual wellbeing.

Care is not asking how you feel or how your weekend was. Care is understanding why an individual is behaving the way they do, and how their current state is standing in the way of their aspirations. Care adds value to the understanding of the current issues and empowers us to achieve higher results. Connect before offering care.

5

Hope in diversity

Strength lies in differences, not in similarities.

Stephen R. Covey

The Nufuth Desert, 2011: Day Three

We need to usher the camels back to their pen. Usually, camels are left to roam, and they tend to go to the far reaches of the surrounding desert. They are good at finding their way home without guidance. Bandar has come by because, this time, a few camels in a neighbouring pasture have strayed too far. To save the situation, he has to get in his car and ride out to meet them.

Two human envoys to the camel colony. I am secretly thankful to be in a car again, a relic of civilisation. It feels like cheating a little bit, but then I remind myself that the point is not to deprive myself of comfort when it arrives. Abu Bandar's son does not know how much of a saviour he is right now. I had been dreading another night alone without human connection.

I previously had no idea that camels could be so stubborn. The trick with camels is that they need a firm hand. You cannot whistle to a camel or slap its rump in order to get it to do what you need it to. Bandar goes so far as bumping them gently with the front of his car in order to coax them to move.

'This doesn't hurt the animal?' I ask.

'No. It gets them to move their lazy asses.'

Some camels get the hint when they see the car approaching and begin to move their legs. Others wait for a few nudges from the car just to show us who's boss and that they were moving anyway.

I am struck by the differences between camels and sheep. It makes me wonder about leadership methods. Sheep are compliant with their leader. They listen. They're easily trained. Camels, on the other hand, are pig-headed.

I compare this with people and their differences. When to be firm or soft? How to motivate? How to connect and show care? Should leaders change their styles?

Abram is a servant leader of the sheep, but my assumption is that Bandar is an autocratic leader of the camels. Bandar is a shepherd as well, and he doesn't treat sheep the way he treats camels. Do leaders learn a style, or do people create a certain style in leaders?

At DAT school, I was told that I am the servant-leader type. I connected and cared about the team, the teachers at the time, while being firm in regards to deadlines and targets. One year during my experience leading the teacher-licensing project, our team increased to twelve members. Issues within the team started to arise, and every other day I was meeting a member who was complaining about work or a colleague. There was definitely an issue, beside the overload of work. I decided to run two personal assessments, behavioural and skills assessment, for each member, followed by team-building training. I wanted the team to know each other better, and to restore the positive culture in the team while setting a new direction.

I was struck by the team's reports. While I thought I was still the servant leader I had been at the school, the team described me as the strong-willed, serious and controlling, and makes-it-happen person in the team. I thought I was more of the listening, supportive and compassionate type, especially after hearing complaints for weeks.

Our coach later explained the reasons why, saying that I had adapted to the team and the project objectives or difficulties. Yet, I still believe that I was a servant leader to the wider body of teachers in the licensing project. I guess I have a thing for the teachers!

I would like to note, at the risk of sounding like a privileged city-slicker, that lunch so far has been exactly the same, every single day. The items on the food tray are not even arranged differently. Two bananas and an apple on the left side of the round aluminium tray. The bananas are always an inch away from ripe and the apple an inch away from rotting. There's also a plastic plate of chicken and rice.

Every day at noon, Abu Bandar's son comes in a timely manner. Sometimes he leaves the tray on my bed if he arrives when the flock and I are still on our way back.

I'm not opposed to the idea of eating the same thing every day during this experiment. I really am not. I am not here for gastronomical pleasure, but I find it astonishing that this tray of food is what Abu Bandar's family has every single day of their lives.

I thank Bandar for his family's generosity, sending me food for the past three days, telling him it was a lot of effort on their part, but he shakes his head and extends a hand to stop me.

'It's what we eat every day. We're just offering you the same,' he says.

I swallow my words of gratitude and continue to be grateful silently. I am glad that Bandar did not hear me commenting to myself about how simple his family's life must be, not to worry about 'what's on the menu'. Is it that their life is hard and they can't afford the luxury of varying the items in their daily meals? Or is it that their life is simply . . . simple, not caring for the luxury of varying their diet? Or is it that my perspective on meals is exaggerated?

I peel my second banana and mull it over. I know for sure that I could not eat the same thing every day, not even for a month.

I asked myself, are other parts of this family's life also consistent? Meaning that if Bandar woke up in the morning, expecting his day to be exactly as the day before, exactly as it has been for the past six months or year, he would probably be absolutely fine with that. Is his whole life really blessed with such a lack of complexity? Does this make his life richer or poorer?

Bandar told me a story when we were going to herd the camels. I don't know why he decided to open up to me. I'm not used to people I don't know well being comfortable enough to open their box of private things and show them to me, but this young man was very cheerful about it. He was driving with one hand on the wheel, the other picking his teeth. With the air of someone clearing his dusty conscience, he said to me:

'This is just between you and me.'

Uh-oh, he did something terrible. I wondered what could this wiry police officer who lives in this godforsaken place be feeling so guilty about that he's using this hushed and remorseful tone. Did he arrest someone he shouldn't have? Did he embezzle?

No, he was on his honeymoon when he did this guilty thing. He was in Egypt with his newly acquired wife. They were having lunch at a restaurant when, all at once, an attractive young woman passed by.

'And you know the women don't cover up in Egypt!' he said.

'Yeah?'

'I looked at her. I found her very attractive.'

'Yeah?'

I waited for the rest of the story. But that was it.

So Bandar carries guilt because he felt attracted to another woman on his honeymoon, and he eats the same lunch every day with his family. Simple, yes? Now I'm not here to judge people's ideologies or lifestyles, but it does strike me as a hassle-free life, both mentally and physically. What I wonder is, does this life bring these people more joy than, say, my way of life ever could? I also wonder, was it our differences that alerted me to notice such a thing? Or was it my ignorance about their culture?

Jeddah, Saudi Arabia, 2013

I feel that Ustaz M. M. is attacking me as new principal for the school. At times, I have found that I can be defensive, and respond with a defence strategy. But I remember that I could not defend nor attack the flock when they ran away from me: I had no choice but to live with the situation. So I do not take M. M.'s attacks personally, and try to see things from his perspective. The school has had many changes in the past few years, and there is no reason to trust a young professional with no previous experience in running a school.

So I realise that he has raised a valid question. What have I ever done to earn the position of principal? What he doesn't know is that while I have not ascended the educational ladder rung by rung, I have climbed the spiral stair of leadership. I came with good will to make changes, but only I believe that, and I have no basis from which to transfer this belief to him. I need to connect further.

My experience as a leader started when I was very young, in my grandfather's house in Makkah – which is often spelled Mecca in English.

We only visited that house once a year in Ramadan. Every year, my grandmother brought with her a host of housekeepers to clean the house from top to bottom to remove the dust and stale air. The sheets were aired thoroughly, although the maids could do nothing to remove the consequences of all the months of abandonment from those sheets. They smelled like any sheets would smell if they had been sweating in a stuffy closet all year.

Our extended family would arrive in groups throughout the last ten days of the month of Ramadan to be present for prayer at the Holy Mosque. While the adults were there for worship, we, the band of kids, were there for the house. It was a mausoleum that was becoming decrepit and that my grandfather had filled with so many wonders that no longer worked. It had its own fountains, dry as your mouth when you wake up in the morning. It had its own cave in the backyard which we 'discovered' and 'explored' every time we visited, only to find the same old spiders and geckos. In the entrance hall, my grandfather had strung a long, retro chandelier that dropped from the third-storey ceiling almost to the floor of the entrance hall. The house was covered entirely in green-brown marble, like the wet skin of a salamander. In retrospect, that marble was hideous, but we thought it was the grandest thing as we ran around the house barefoot, cooling the soles of our feet. And it made for the best surface for sliding down the stairs on mattresses.

As we ran around all over the large house playing make-believe, we preferred the basement for our best games because, down there, we did not get in the way of the adults and were, therefore, never scolded.

The basement was the stalest part of the house. The carpet there was so old that the weave had stuck together and trapped the smell of hookah smoke between its threads. There was a pool down there encircled with glass walls. There were chairs that we could stack together to build cockpits and fly our planes across the world.

My favourite game was the 'business game'. It was very simple. We had a business, and I was the CEO. I distributed the roles to my cousins according to what they were best at. We didn't really know what our business was about, but what thrilled us, as children, was the idea of having a role in something. I must have invented documents to be signed and speeches to be given, but they all belonged to this abstract idea of what the adult world was like. I do remember that I thoroughly liked being the responsible one.

As children, before we are made aware of the truths of the world we live in, we can easily let authority get to our heads because it reminds us of the authority and control that our parents have over us. It was exhilarating for me to experience that authority. I was always the boss in this game, and the others seemed happy to let me take that part. At least, I hope they were!

About ten years later, I was walking down the corridor in the campus at King Fahad University. As a college student, I was excited about all the opportunities that the campus made available for me to flex my opportunist muscles. I was looking for something new to do.

I overheard some professors say that the Environmental Design Club was closing down because it had been inactive for three years. When I asked if I could be the president of the club, I was told I would not be accepted because I was a sophomore – in my second year at university.

So I marched right into the Student Affairs Office and requested to be made the president of the club. They had a different reason for objecting.

'It's closing down,' said the tired old Student Affairs officer.

'That's why I'm here. I want to keep it running.'

'I'm sorry. We can't offer that position to you because the club has been inactive for too long. We can't waste space and resources on it any more. There are other clubs you can join.'

'Listen,' I said, 'I am full of energy, and I want to put it into bringing that club back to life. Before you close it down, why not give me a chance?'

The officer looked at me sceptically. Then he referred me to a higher-up, something authorities in bureaucratic environments tend to do when they don't feel like dealing with a persistent person like me.

I eventually made a convincing case. I became the president of a club that had around eighty – very inactive – members.

At the club's reopening, for which I had reserved a venue and prepared some inspirational fliers, I waited until late evening for someone to show up. No one came. It was a huge let-down for me to be so ignored, even by my friends, after I had fought my way through upper management to keep the club open.

My resolve gathered itself again. By the time I had given up on my expectations that anyone would show, I was already planning a second try. Only this time, there would be *food*. I sent out dinner invitations to the existing club members. They came – not all of them, but enough to kick-start the club again.

As we moved forward, campaigning and designing projects all around campus, the club flourished, and our numbers grew so that we had more members than there were students in the School of Architectural Design. We had over a hundred.

We made our work fun. We put in late nights in our headquarters, designing various campus projects and events. I learned more than I imagined I could about being a leader.

Well, maybe I was born to be a leader, but the DAT teachers don't appreciate that. For them there is one sticking point: *I have never worked in a school*. I understand Ustaz M. M.'s doubts. It is only natural to wonder: can a person lead a group when he knows very little about what the people do? Can he lead others who have no reason to trust him? And of course there's the underlying question: What did I do to merit becoming their leader, and why on earth should they follow me?

During my first few weeks in the school, I spend time making rounds and getting to know everyone, from the janitors to the department heads. I sit down for a friendly chat with each and every person until my mind becomes a collage of their life stories. In speaking to me, a cheerful twenty-nine-year-old, many find an opportunity to express their professional, and personal, concerns.

One afternoon, I sit with the head of the high-school division. It becomes a two-hour conversation in his office about work, life and his children, one of whom turns out to be the same age as I am.

He seems relaxed, eager and willing to work with me. I sit back watching him recall his last trip to Egypt with a fond smile on his face. I realise that if I have managed to get the head of the high-school division to work with me, then I have rallied a worthy ally in the mission towards reform.

Our conversation begins to dissipate, and it feels like it's time to go. I get up and thank him for his time. He stands in response and says the usual polite things when you're about to show a guest out.

He walks me to the door and I expect to leave his office solo, but he follows me instead. He walks me all the way to the door of the high-school building. Well, that's kind of him, I think.

Later, I catch on to the meaning of that gesture. It was not about being a good host. He was not so riveted by our conversation that he wanted to carry on with it all the way to the door of the building. He was marking his territory.

Some disagreements begin to arise between the two of us as we start to work through the school term. I learn that he does not want me to speak to his teachers without his permission, or visit his classes without his prior knowledge, which of course, as headmaster of the school, it is my right and my job to do. We have issues to work out.

6

The emptiness of the desert resets everything

Become totally empty. Quiet the restlessness of the mind.
Only then will you witness everything unfolding from emptiness.

Lao Tzu

The Nufuth Desert, 2011: Day Three

The moon is a fascinating orb. You cannot look enough at the moon, and when you look away it's only because you're overwhelmed by its perfection. A common phrase in Arabic is what I can best translate as 'a fourteenth moon'. The fourteenth day in every lunar month, according to the Islamic calendar, is when the moon is at its fullest and brightest. In Arab culture, beautiful women are often described as 'fourteenth moons'.

I'm thinking about how the emptiness and vastness of the desert resets everything I know about the world. If I were like Abram, and spent all my days out here in the middle of nowhere taking care of these vulnerable beasts, I would not be a part of the world. That means I would not be aware of the news. I would not be updated on the latest technologies. If someone showed me the oldest version of Nintendo, I would think it was genius. I wouldn't know much about this mad, charging, grasping thing called modern civilisation.

And yet I *would* be a part of the world. I would be part of the world that has been here before any of us. It's strange how we think we created our world, as if there was nothing in existence before us. The funny thing is, if we were wiped off the earth, it would continue to go on without us. I suddenly feel the might of our planet, and my respect for Abram deepens. To surrender to this organised and chaotic force that is our planet is the bravest thing a human being can do.

I sit up on my bed in the middle of the night, around 3 a.m. Everything is quiet. The sheep wheeze in their sleep. I stare directly into the full moon. I am struck by the sudden oneness that I feel out here. The sky and the earth are one, aside from the moonlit distance where the thin line of the horizon can barely be recognised. The tops of the sand dunes catch the light on their humps. There is no noise, not even in my own mind. I have found silence in there, too.

I have never before experienced such unadulterated and absolute peace.

Even silence has a sound. It's like a roll of thick fabric being unrolled from the spool endlessly, for miles, to infinity. At night I tune in to the silence as the sound of the universe breathing. I think about how the big silence out there is stitching our moments together. Between every occurrence on Planet Earth, there is silence. Before beginning there is silence, and after all is done, there is silence.

I start my day earlier than the sheep because I need to bring their food and fill up their water tank using a hose that pulls water from the well. I end my day after they end theirs because I must clean up after them once they've settled down to sleep at night. This makes my day longer, and I'm surprised every time I drop down on my hard bed how tired I am.

I really thought I would be sitting around on the sand and contemplating the universe. But it turns out that this is real labour. It's even more labour when you've been chasing the sheep all day in thick sand. I am their silence, the one that connects the dots that they cannot connect on their own.

So I am grateful every night when it is time to rest. I drop into sleep like a deep, dark chasm, and I wake up like clockwork just before the sun rises. I think this is how we all should sleep. The labour is hard, but gratifying, and the exhaustion is just a bonus. If during the day I feel so alive, with every cell whirring with joy, sleep feels like the sweetest death that just snatches the rug from under my feet, and I gladly fall.

I ponder about things before I sleep, though. I have a small window for those thoughts that start to connect. I never appreciated walls in my life. I have no walls around me out here, nothing to protect me from the elements. I am impressed by the idea of walls. It's only God and me. Really. For the past four days, I've been aware of that. Anything could happen to me out here. I could even get swallowed by the night by mistake. I could disappear from existence. So I cling to God. I take that with me to sleep, but not before I long for the comforting sounds of sirens in Cambridge. Humans rushing to rescue one another. Humans rushing to keep everyone else safe.

Only me and God. I close my eyes and surrender.

The Nufuth Desert, 2011: Day Four

Before dawn I wake up again, this time not in peace but in panic. There's a wolf near the pen.

Shapes in the dark are sometimes larger when seen with a bleary eye. Sounds, when you hover between sleep and waking, seem more threatening. The shape that I see is the figure of a dog, and the sound that I hear is its growl.

I learn this morning that this is the shepherd's dog from the neighbouring camel pasture. It occasionally makes a visit here to 'supervise'.

When I jumped from bed earlier today and grabbed my staff – did I mention I have a staff? – I was ready to charge at the 'wolf' with a vocally aggressive rant. I don't know what I would have done, really, if it *had* been a wolf. Would I have sacrificed myself for the sheep?

But the truth of the matter is that the dog was protecting the sheep from *me*. To its canine nose and dog instincts, I was the stranger, the predator.

Now I feel foolish. I consider telling everyone it was a wolf, just to colour the story a bit.

I decide to make friends with the dog. You know when you meet a group of people who have been friends for a long time and they don't seem inclined to let you in at first, and your search hones in on the nice guy? That is the dog. I think the dog is like an opinion leader: win the dog and I will have access to the flock.

Abram taught the dog this morning that I am not the enemy. But this dog is loyal to the flock. I might have to pass a couple of tests before we establish any bonds. Bribery, I think, always works with animals. So I save a piece of chicken from my lunch as a friendship offering.

I inch closer to the dog as he sits with his paws extended like the great sphinx, guarding the flock as it takes its midday slurp of water.

Like any well-wishing human who seeks to be friends with an animal, I start to make all sorts of silly noises: clucking, whistling, hissing. The dog ignores me.

Abram looks up over a bale of dry grass. We have now established a junkyard of gestures and sounds as our means of communication. I point at the dog.

'What's his name?' I blurt in the hope that he might pick up a word or two.

'Nada,' he says. He stares at me for a second and then goes back to work. My fascination with the dog is not entertaining to him.

The dog, it turns out, is a fast runner. He will sprint across the sand to the farthest point in sight where a sheep has strayed, to bring it back with a snap of his jaw. He pounces on snakes and swiftly finishes them off. He sometimes drags the bales of dry grass into the pen. All with that frail but quick body.

As another attempt to befriend the dog, I decide to drop all pretence.

No bribery, no hesitation. I crouch down in front of him and look him in the eye. He barks at me. I extend an open palm for him to sniff.

He drops his nose close to my skin. He looks at me.

I can smell it all right. Now how can I help you?

I sit there with my palm extended for what must be five minutes. He sniffs some more, then turns away. I notice that his muscles have relaxed. He puts his head between his paws and goes half to sleep.

My connection to Nada fails; we are not friends, even if he no longer believes that I am a threat. I am driven by one mission, to experience shepherding and connect with the flock. I have tried multiple times to connect with the flock, but I am still that monster around them, from whom they run in the opposite direction. Maybe I am desperate? Well, that's a wish I never thought I desired, to connect with a flock! I do not take the time or put in the effort to connect to Nada because I am focusing on the flock. Among all the animals around me, my attention is directed to the sheep. Do I not care about the dog? I don't want to admit that is the reason why we do not connect.

Sometimes, our will and focus on an issue deviates us away from our wider purpose out of frustration at not achieving what we want; we quit so quickly that we do not let our learning curve grow gradually to make results happen. Yet, every problem has more than one solution. Nada could be the route to connect with the flock.

The dog is the protector of the sheep: if the flock considers Nada the safety zone, then I could be safe to safety, so I could be safe to the flock too. But I have not pursued that route clearly. I am trying to make the connection happen through the stubborn sheep.

I am failing.

Jeddah, Saudi Arabia, 2013

'How is your wife, Mr S. D.?' I ask.

'How did you know?'

He did not expect the school principal to remember. Or to care.

'We're all one big family now, aren't we?' I say. 'So how is she?'

'She is doing well. She gave birth to a baby boy and named him AlBaraa, after you.'

My heart leaps between happiness and gratitude. My voice fails me, and I lose the words to respond.

'We hope he will be like you, Ustaz AlBaraa,' he adds.

After a moment, I am able to speak.

'I pray for him to be a better man,' I say.

Being recognised inspires me. It really moves me

to have a child named after me but, honestly, I fear these moments the most. The moments when I am rewarded for an accomplishment or celebrating a successful project. I feel that the emotional peak of joy will downgrade my emotional will to continue. Yes, I have been told before many times that I am giving myself a hard time. I am trying to celebrate moments of joy. By contrast, being ignored ignites other feelings. Feelings I want ignited.

I once attended a symposium with an education consultation committee. It was headed by a member of the royal family in Saudi Arabia. There were VIPs present from ministries and municipalities, and they had invited college students and young people such as me as a gesture of inclusion. They needed our creative problem-solving skills, but they didn't need them that much.

I had thoughts, I had ideas, but I felt like only a head in the crowd that day. I was furiously writing in my notebook and, at the same time, reminding myself that we were invited here to speak up. I couldn't help noticing, though, that many of the senior speakers did not look our way.

The vice minister of the Ministry of Economy and Planning gave his presentation about the kingdom's struggles with education, pointing out that a single student costs the government 55,000 riyals per year (about £11,000/US$15,000).

When the microphone was passed around in the discussion afterwards, I raised my hand. At the time, I was a little timid about sharing my thoughts in public, and was only prepared to do so after writing my questions and thoughts down and reviewing them at least ten times. I put forward a suggestion to ease the struggle with education expenditure. My idea was that, since public school was free and deteriorating because of lack of attention and care, all schools should be made private, with the government subsidising full tuition and focusing its efforts on managing education. My idea was to relieve the financial burden from government agencies and to inject responsibility and accountability into the public. Regardless of whether this suggestion was wise, informed or even worth uttering, it was my way of engaging with the problem at hand, and I felt called to speak because I was a member of the youth who were invited. My suggestion was overlooked. The vice minister barely gave me a glance and then moved on to the next person with a question. I sat there for the remainder of the discussion wallowing in embarrassment and fury that I had been ignored.

My point is that I know what it is like to be made to feel invisible. I can imagine what it feels like to be made invisible over the course of an entire career.

So I look at Ustaz M. M. and see my moment of invisibility multiplied into thousands of days. Through the quiet manner in which he spoke to me, I am able to hear the edges of his rage.

The sheep don't know how to choose their pasture or the easiest path to it. The sand here can be tricky because in some areas it's so soft that your foot can sink a couple of feet with every step you take, which means more muscle work. Where the dunes are wavy, the sand is more compact and allows for more solid footing. A good shepherd guides the sheep through the path that won't tire them out and to the nearest and greenest pasture. There is no need to overwork the sheep.

Today I realise that they have begun to recognise me, but only in the afternoon. I've made it my task to be the one to open the gate for them for their second feeding, and they've begun to respond. *Oh, okay. This is the man who opens the gate for us now.* They amble past me, and I feel a proud grin spread in childlike glee across my face. They're beginning to know me. When the last one is out, I close the gate and do a little dance.

This desert has stripped me of everything I know and every comfort I thought I could not live without (such as a fully charged iPhone). But this small progress makes the road ahead a little clearer. I had been beginning to wonder if all of this meant nothing, and if I would go home with a failed experiment. At least I can say now that I was persistent enough for the sheep to recognise me during the afternoon.

Shepherding is starting to grow on me.

7

Ready to face challenges again

When we least expect it, life sets us a challenge to test our courage and willingness to change; at such a moment, there is no point in pretending that nothing has happened or in saying that we are not yet ready. The challenge will not wait. Life does not look back.

Paulo Coelho

The Nufuth Desert, 2011: Day Four

No snakes yet.

As I walk along the sand dunes, though, I see those tracks dusting the surface and suddenly I'm reminded of that old computer game, *Minesweeper*. What if I am surrounded by snakes, but I just haven't stepped on one yet?

I live in fear every day of dehydration and poisoning. Abu Bandar made sure of that. It's becoming part of my daily regimen. I wake up in the morning, and these are the first two thoughts that pop into my mind's radio station.

They say that fear weakens the body. I wonder what shepherds around the world have feared before me. Taking out livestock into some form of desolation, being responsible for yourself and the entire herd, to protect them and yourself from whatever threat could pose itself. Let the geography determine that: deserts, tundra, fields surrounded by wolves.

What could a shepherd in the Alps be fearing, for example? When the meadows and the mountain slopes are green in the summer and the weather is pleasant, what does he fear? Slippery slopes? Nightfall on the slippery slopes? Or perhaps nothing? What if the only fear that a shepherd in such an ideal location has is the complete removal of his identity as he dedicates his days to the livestock from dawn to dusk? Or maybe that *is* his identity.

I find myself compelled to think grandiose thoughts as I go out shepherding. I try to think the same thoughts that Koranic prophets thought. They must have thought about God and the vastness of the sky and the nature of Nature. But then I wonder if any one of them perhaps broke the leather on his sandal one day and had to limp across the desert for hours until it was time to go home. I wonder if one dreaded going home to a wife who did not understand him, or if one had social anxiety, or felt lost or bored. I wonder if any one of them dreaded greatness so much that he would have been terrified to know that his name would one day be eternally recorded in a holy book.

So I stop trying to think grandiose thoughts and resume thinking my own everyday thoughts. My thesis. My aeroplane ride home. The comments I will be getting about my harshly acquired tan.

I see a snake!

The Nufuth Desert, 2011: Day Five

I broke my staff this morning. In the Koran, Moses mentions his staff, which he uses for myriad things, only one of which is to tend the herd. One of his uses I find most interesting: he mentions that he props himself up on it. My mind searches for a metaphor here. Even leaders need support. Moses was reputed to be tall, wide, physically agile and strong, but even a man with a build like that must have needed support every now and then.

I used my staff to dig into the sand and prop myself up as I hiked over the dunes. I didn't really use it to tap the sheep into movement because they still don't let me anywhere near them. They start to run as soon as I approach, so I'm like a shepherd's staff myself. But I did have a vain sense of comfort just holding it. It was a prop that I felt I needed. So I start to wonder about how things can invoke in us a sense of validation or confidence.

I needed the sense of validation to assure myself I am experiencing the authentic way. I needed a staff, a stubborn flock, and the heat. Functionally the staff was useful, but emotionally it was more helpful.

The staff offered me confidence, although I could walk on the sand without this prop. It was like a plan B: I always knew the staff would be there if I fell.

In college, my father bought me a car, a common gift from a father to his kids when they go to college. After two years, I decided to sell it and buy a small amount of real estate. I wanted to get into that business. When I travelled to the USA for my master's, I left the business, never visited 'my land'. I would not say that I benefited from it. On the contrary, I spent a lot of money to buy it, and sacrificed my freedom of mobility. What I received was more valuable than mobility and cash, however, it was the confidence and stability. I always knew that I had a plan B waiting for me in case I failed in life. I would sell the land and start over.

This confidence and stability increased my risk taking. George Kohlrieser, a leading psychologist, hostage negotiator and professor of leadership at the International Institute for Management Development (IMD) in Switzerland, calls this a 'secure base'. In his book, *Hostage at the Table*, he explains that 'secure bases come in many forms. They are primarily people; parents, grandparents, teachers, coaches, bosses, friends, colleagues, and so on. They can also be countries, pets, goals, beliefs, or religion.' I had the honour of taking the High Performance Leadership course with Kohlrieser, and learned how a secure base, something as negligible as a staff, can improve self-esteem and confidence, but more importantly it will keep a shepherd focused on the goal, as his mindset is secured against issues that might arise if he did not have a staff. 'A secure base gives protection or comfort and is a source of energy. If there is danger, we turn to our secure bases,' he explains. On the contrary, Kohlrieser continues, 'if we lose a secure base, our emotional balance can dramatically change, and in the turmoil, the immense significance of the secure base becomes apparent'.

The staff was my secure base. Abram is still a secure base. Probably the flock's rejection of me is another secure base as a shepherd-in-training: they are pushing me to try ways to learn. What will I do if they accept me?!

I've been feeling something accumulating under my skin that I wish was not there. It's been amassing for days and, if I'm not mistaken, I would say it's a storm of exasperation.

I leaned on my broken staff this morning, just like Moses did, as I watched the lazy sheep leave the pen without a glance my way. It's day five, and already I'm starting to feel very tired with this lifestyle, with the isolation. It's not like the sheep are showing significant signs of yielding. I looked around in disgust this morning at my own choice to be here. I felt tired of shedding more and more clothing every day in the heat. On my first day of shepherding I was in a proud pair of jeans with nothing on my head. Today I'm down to shorts and a sleeveless undershirt. I loathe whoever thought sleeves were ever necessary. My overshirt is instead tied around my head as a turban to keep my scalp from scalding in the sun because the original piece of cloth I had was too flimsy to protect it.

The harshness of the surroundings has set in, the odour of the sheep, the scarcity of water and moisture, the hard bed and my constant alertness for danger. It's tough.

So I leaned on that stick for support during my five days in this desert. The experience is weighing heavily on me. And that was probably what broke it.

This afternoon, I'm out with the sheep in the pasture with no staff. I look around with contempt at this arid land. What does it feed these sheep, exactly? What does this land offer to these creatures every single day? What could be new? What could be fresh? How important are these sheep anyway? How much money do they bring in? How do they really serve their owners?

Without a staff, I climb these mountains like a cripple. I feel like I have lost a limb instead of a piece of wood. I picked that staff carefully from a lucky little valley on my first day. I felt like quite the shepherd, indeed. I felt legitimate. Serious.

I scan the area all around. There is no stick to match it. I pick up one wooden rod, but it's eaten up in all sorts of places. This other stick is too thin, another too gnarly; I can't keep a comfortable grip around it.

So I wander around staffless for hours. I sit on the hot sand, pushing down the one thought I did not want to think about all morning, that one roaring thought – so loud you would need a large boulder to sit on top of it to shut it up. And even then you would still hear its murmur.

I'm failing.

A reasonable voice rises timidly and says: it's only been five days. You have five more to go.

Five more of what? Of this? What is this?

I know the road to success has many failures, I believe in that, but it sounds so theoretical to me now. I am in no place for a pep talk and motivational speeches. It is hot, it is dry, I stink, I have no idea where I am, it is day five and I'm still rejected by the animals. Fact is, I am expecting difficulties, and Abu Bandar prepared me to expect the worse, death. Even though I am so tired. I am sitting between these dunes looking at burned barrels that look to be oil tanks. The harshness of the situation deludes me into seeing what is not there. I think that these barrels could be the remnants of a felony or a crime scene. Who was here? Why did they have to burn these barrels? Was it only barrels or did they use gas to burn what is no longer visible . . . a body?

I feel that failure is getting into me, especially after this crazy thought of a burned body. I remember that a tiny negative incident in the morning can cripple a whole day. One day, I woke up twenty minutes late and missed the first ten minutes of an important meeting. On my way to the meeting, I felt that cars were stopping purposefully in front of me, delaying me even more. My frustration was gradually growing because of a snoozed alarm. In the meeting, I missed a few important points at the beginning, so nothing made sense. My nerves were on edge. After the meeting, a colleague came to my office, and I responded with frustration and I injured our relationship. And so there I was, irritated and standing on the edge of a nervous breakdown just because of a snoozed alarm.

'STOP,' I scream to myself out loud. 'We have been here for five days and even the animals do not accept you,' I rationally respond to the voices inside my head. The failure of not connecting with the sheep is eating me alive, and I am not acting rationally. I remember when Bandar challenged me to survive one night, I remember the death warnings from Abu Bandar. 'I'd agree that you should continue if you had made progress in connecting with the sheep. Up until today, the fifth day, the sheep are not getting any closer and the dog has rejected your friendship, Abram can't speak Arabic or English, you haven't had a shower, your family is worried, and there is a chance that people were burned alive just a few metres from where you are standing.'

The voice telling me that I am failing is gaining strength and I feel my muffling boulder begin to lift involuntarily. All at once, I feel like screaming or kicking those sheep in their woolly butts.

The boulder lifts completely now, and the feeling rises before I can contain it. I stand and throw a rock at one of the sheep.

It turns to me and moans.

'That didn't hurt? Come! Come on, I'm wide open!'

The sheep only looks at me, chewing with two mundane jaws. It turns away and then dips its head down for another chew.

I pick up another rock. Then I drop to the ground, ashamed of myself. If Abu Bandar could see me throwing rocks at his flock! Some shepherd I am.

I have got to get a grip on myself. I look around at every one of the sheep in sight. All I see is dumbness. Just the way they hang their heads as they chew, the way they shiver their bodies to tease the flies away, their lazy pace and their blank stares. I might have had better luck with horses. With camels, I might have had some excitement working through their stubbornness. But what do you do with a flock that barely recognises you? It's not the sheep's fault they're dumb creatures. Although, speaking of dumb, I'm glad I wasn't enough of an idiot to throw a rock at that male with horns.

I'm behaving like a child with a tantrum. I think I'll go look again for another staff. Honestly, it felt good releasing that anger by throwing a rock. It felt like letting out the pain of failure. I'm still ashamed though.

■ ■ ■

At the Environmental Design Club, we worked so hard as one family to achieve so much that had never been done before. Eventually, we were ranked the best club in the entire university. The Student Affairs officer did not regret his decision to approve my presidency application, until one day after the summer vacation of my junior year.

I had been handling the club's treasury generously. By that, I mean I was constantly looking for opportunities to save the money allotted to us by the university so that I could get extra things for the team, such as a decent TV screen for our small office. Or I would try to accumulate funds for the extra projects we were excited about but could not pursue because of a shortage in the treasury. So I saved up ten riyals here, a hundred there, and kept them stored in cash in various hiding places in our headquarters. I stashed the notes in pots and hid them inside books to keep the money safe for when the need arose.

When I came back from summer vacation, the money was gone. We could not find it in our headquarters. It had vanished from all the hiding places that I knew so well.

There was a lot of talk, as there is bound to

be after a fiasco such as this, and the talk was eventually directed at me. I was accused of stealing the money.

This club was the highlight of my accumulating experience as a leader. I valued my position because we were getting work done and we were having immense fun doing it. It was a time when I really began to value myself and my capabilities. To say I was heartbroken would have been an overstatement, but I definitely felt betrayed. I had given my team my trust, and they had given me theirs. To have that snatched away in a matter of days created a significant shift in my awareness. Trust is a fragile thing, so fragile that I had even lost any heart to defend myself to the team. There was no longer any point. After the turmoil had calmed down a bit, I heard from the team that they were ready to 'forgive' me.

I announced to Student Affairs at the university that I was disappointed by the accusations. I could not tell them that something inside me was crumbling, or that I could no longer see myself taking on a team of this size again, or that this was the worst experience I had endured as a college student. But I did tell them that I was going to complete our current project as I had promised and that, after that, I would resign from my post as club president. Not because I was the culprit, not because I resented my accusers, but because the trust of my peers and superiors had disappeared. I could not work with people who expected the worst of me when I had done the best for them and with them.

It took me a while to rebuild my trust in trust. In 2006, still a student, I organised a group trip to a local orphanage to play with the orphans. The group grew larger organically as we recruited more team members, and the work we did was the most rewarding I had ever done. Because of that trip, I later founded a community service organisation, Live4Umma (*umma* in Arabic means 'nation'), that managed various charity events in Jeddah and many awareness campaigns. At one time the organisation had over a thousand members in eight different countries. Today, Live4Umma is my secure base, what I turn to for confidence and comfort.

On days when I feel like I haven't done anything of use to society – and those days are many – I google 'Live4Umma' just to remind myself that a single, well-intentioned action can easily ripple out and move an entire part of the world.

I remember this experience as I lie awake in the desert. Persevering and embracing risk saw me through the challenge. Well, I'm certainly risking my life out here. Maybe if I persevere, I can still learn some wisdom from these sheep. It seems like a hopeless plan at this point, but so did the plan for success at the Environmental Design Club. I drop off to sleep, rededicating myself to persevering and seeing my mission through.

8

Redefining failure

All of this abundance begins to shine through a mind that is aware of its own infinite nature. There's enough for everyone. See it. Believe it. It will show up for you.

Rhonda Byrne

The Nufuth Desert, 2011: Day Five

I rethink my assumption. Are sheep *really* dumb?

Don't get me wrong. I am not likening human beings to sheep, but I have often felt the same frustration I feel with these animals when working with a group that refused to understand my position on something, or with whom communication was a challenge.

When I was doing my master's, I enjoyed working on group projects. Of course, having the privilege to choose your team is ideal, but that is almost never the case. Usually you find yourself with a diverse group of people with different nationalities. American and Chinese students were the two dominant nationalities on the Boston campus. Other nationalities each made up less than 5 per cent. Because of this, the mix did not feel diverse at all, but I tried to fit in. Working in groups was challenging for me. At first, communicating with our Chinese colleagues was difficult. We could not understand each other. This crippled our communication during our project work. But then I reflected that this was probably how the American students felt about me as well. When arguments were made, communication suffered because we did not have an even level of understanding on which we could base our discussions. The experience taught me how lacking I am in communication skills.

So you see, this makes me wonder if the sheep really are as dumb as they seem. What if the problem is my own thinking? Putting human intelligence and sheep intelligence aside, what remains between us is needs. I have needs, and so do they. It is only a matter of who fulfils those needs for the other the fastest. Or who has been fulfilling those needs already for years. How can I make the sheep come to me for their needs instead of Abram? Well, Abram would have to go, of course, if that were really my objective here. But Abram is not going anywhere, and I don't want him to.

For the sake of argument, though, let's just say that Abram is leaving the flock entirely to me. That he's getting on some airline to go visit his family and maybe will never come back. Let's just say that I'm the boss of these sheep.

I predict that some of them would die. The animals have depended for years on the one person who could save them from any threat, even if it was only a tick. To be left with a clueless guy like me would be a threat in itself. Coming to think about it, I totally understand how they feel about me now: a threat. To the flock, I am change, with lots of risk. They have the choice not to follow me because Abram is there caring for each sheep. I have to work hard to care as much as Abram does. So this means that in order for me to be as good as Abram at shepherding this particular flock – as opposed to any other flock – I would need time, more time than ten days, to get to know their specific and individual needs, to learn to recognise each of them instantly. They would have to trust me completely for the sake of their survival. My conclusion is that I may have been pushing myself too hard. Maybe my goal or my expectations have been too high, or maybe my expectations were selfish, focusing on me not dying from a stupid snake or dehydration. I wanted to shepherd, I wanted to connect and care, but my mind wanted to survive. Maybe I need more time. In ten days, maybe all I need to be able to manage is to get their attention.

I find a staff. It's not as theatrical as the old one that broke, but I'm happy enough with it, and it keeps me supported as I climb these slippery hills.

My life is adding up now, moment to moment. I used to swallow it in days and weeks and months, thinking, *Where did all that time go?*

Moment to moment, hill to hill, sheep to sheep, sunrise to sunset. I've acquired a new meaning of time here. Everything else now seems so foreign to me. How do you live your life in that mindless daze anyway? Why do you do it? I've been asking myself these questions ever since I got here.

I'm in the car with Bandar. He has the simplicity of country folk anywhere in the world and the heart of a daredevil. Or so it seems to me because I'm not used to driving around at night in the middle of the desert without a single light on and with no particular care for potholes in the sand.

As he races the car and swerves left and right, I catch my breath and my stomach goes for a dive. *I do not want to die tonight! Not this way!* I've survived this long, I keep saying to myself. I survived thirst, heat and those dreaded snakes. I am not about to lose my precious life in this car in what seems to be Bandar's favourite form of entertainment. As he jerks the car left and right, I hold on to the door handle as if it will save me from dying. I try not to think about the four young men who died on a dark highway because they crashed into a strolling camel.

Then I realise what it is exactly that Bandar enjoys. It's the same thing we enjoy when we're blindfolded and told to look for our friends in a game of hide-and-seek. We are not able to see, but we still manage to catch our friends. It's defeating the uncertainty, diving into the unknown without a thing in clear sight and still managing to conquer it, that gives Bandar the thrill.

This brings me back to my own questions. Why do we live in a mindless daze, from high school, through college, onward through our careers? Life feels empty because of our own fear of uncertainty. We cling to what we know, and when the time comes, when we decide to play a little with fire, it clings to us in return. What if you lost your job one day? You would think about your next logical move to stay on the boat of your career. Well, what if you decided to take a year off and collect exotic butterflies instead? How many people would have the courage to make an outlandish choice, even if it's something they have always desired? You might actually want to do that. But what if your fear of uncertainty would not let you go? So you look for job after job on your pre-planned route and never let your toe slip outside of the boat and into the water. So many people make these choices because they are, to their minds, the most certain.

When I was a kid, I was standing in the wake of time, moving from one milestone to another. Finish one school year then move to the next, graduate from high school, then move to college. I did not want to be on this default track for life. School, college, job, marriage, kids, house, retirement, death.

It was only because I thought less of me, when I failed to meet my expectations in college, that I wanted to change. The only constant was me, and time was taking me from one spot to another. I did not control time, it controlled me.

The only constant here is surviving. 'But you tried to connect and care,' I argue with myself. True, I was doing great, but deep inside my priority was to survive.

The only reason I am thinking this way now is failure. Failure nudged my thoughts to question the status quo, to break the constant of time, asking for a behavioural change. I need to change, to translate that failure into positive energy and focus on the flock.

The car jerks to a stop. After a dizzying ride, I open my eyes. I feel like I've been on a boat, cruising through high dunes. I am so thankful to have put my seatbelt on. We're back at our spot apparently. I am shaken now, not just because of the ride, but because of all the certainty that I clung to and that has clung to me all my life.

When I jump out of the car, Bandar turns the headlights on so that I can see the path back to my resting place.

Great. Thanks.

The Nufuth Desert, 2011: Day Six

Still thinking about uncertainty. I wake up at dawn today and notice how the sky looks different than it did yesterday. I realise that it will look different tomorrow. I also realise that I am OK with that.

I don't know what could happen today, or tomorrow, or in a week. For once, I am hyper-aware of the sand against the side of my foot as I step down from my bed. No snakes around. I am alive and grateful. I am hopeful.

The water is cooler today, or maybe I just never noticed it before. My skin tingles around my eyes and behind my ears after I splash it onto my face. The air is still, like it has stopped to watch my every move.

I go to the pen with the sense of something deeper than accomplishment could ever provoke. It's oneness. I am exactly where I'm supposed to be, I realise, not a millimetre short, not a millimetre further.

I feed the sheep and watch them munching as I lean against the railing of the pen. I am suddenly aware that I am not planning my next move. I am simply here with the sheep, and relief rushes over me in a cascade. I don't need anything right now but to watch them. I don't even have to plan the rest of my day.

When I walk towards the gate to open it for the sheep, I feel like my steps are guided today. Or that they are safe wherever they fall. Or that they have fallen in tune. I don't know. Something like that.

I find myself whistling as I watch the sheep march lazily past me towards the pasture. I'm not even complaining about the heat.

How did this come about? My thoughts go back to uncertainty. Have I tricked myself into accepting it?

The sheep take their time moseying between their moisture-deficient snacks. I take my time climbing up the hill, then the next, then the next. I climb so many hills today with newly returned vigour, so much vigour that I finally end up in an empty spot of land with not a single sheep in sight. That's all right. They're only further off behind that sand dune over there. I climb up to the crest, but I don't see the herd.

I look at my water, and I've already drunk half the bottle.

A creeping dread takes over me, and my heart begins to panic. No wait! I climb over the next dune, and the one after that.

Maybe a slight change of direction will do it. I turn a few degrees to the left and keep going that way. Still no herd. Half an hour later, I don't see anything but sand all around me, and it all looks the same.

It's day six, and I am lost.

The sun is high now. It's noon. My face is burning. My body has grown tired of the search and the heat. My bottle is dangerously low on water.

I do not waste my breath crying for help because there is no one here. I continue to tune my ears in to any sound the sheep might be making, but all I hear is the muffled silence continuing forever into space.

How did I come this far? So much for the stillness and tranquillity that I felt this morning. This is where it got me. Overconfidence. I start yelling at myself in my head. I've been in a lull when I should have been worrying about staying alive. I had no business to be exercising. I had no business to be feeling oneness and in-tune-ness and all that nonsense. My heart rises to my throat as one thought reveals itself with a flourish.

'Beware of death.' It's Abu Bandar's voice inside my head.

I find that there is nothing to do but sit down under the grilling sun and rest for a bit. I can hear that thought screaming. I pray that one of the sheep will appear and rescue me.

Another battalion appears in my head that yells at those fears to pipe down because they're not helping. I laugh at myself despite my predicament. What there is to laugh about, I will never know. But my laughing verges on hysterical. I laugh until my bones hurt. For six days I stayed alive in the desert. This was bound to happen in the end, wasn't it? Might as well meet a snake right here. I take a swig of water. What the hell? It's not enough water to last me fifteen minutes anyway.

When I'm done laughing, my stomach hurts, and I realise that my fears have gone quiet. I look around in the space inside my mind and find not a single voice speaking.

Are you guys sure? I ask them. You have nothing else to say?

Not a word. I must have scared them off by laughing. The tranquillity I felt in the morning rushes into their place. Well, if this is not uncertainty then I don't know what is!

I decide to trust. I don't decide, really. It is not a decision. In a predicament like this, something larger than you opens the way to trust despite the danger at hand. I say a small but believing prayer, and I get up again, despite the whining of my muscles and the thud of the sun on my head. I have completely lost my orientation. Here comes Abu Bandar inside my mind: '*and we will not find you*'. I ask myself, 'Is that the beginning of an end?' My heartbeat escalates, and I am starting to shake. Abu Bandar's words eliminated the possibility that I would be rescued by others. I am all alone now. I have no option but to figure out a way to survive. I know for sure, though, that in the circumference around, there are directions I've already eliminated as the right way to go. So I choose a direction that I have not eliminated yet, which is behind me, and I walk that way.

Down the dune I go and up the next. For half an hour I walk straight, climbing up and down the waves of dunes. I am hoping that something will seem familiar, but nothing does. It's almost like the desert is constantly reshaping and repainting itself when we aren't looking.

I am not quitting: it is not an option that I have even considered. I did not sit down earlier because of remorse, I really didn't. It was so I could find a solution and work towards it. Will Smith's 'I either win, or die' is boosting me with confidence and motivation to continue.

Then I see camel-hoof prints! Tracks! Tracks mean guidance. Tracks are the way home. I run diagonally towards them. Unspeakable joy bursts through me. That feeling that you're saved. You don't experience it often in life.

The tracks run down the dunes and up others, and I chase them because my life depends on it. After what feels like an eternity of climbing up and down sand dunes, in fear I will find the tracks ahead of me somehow erased, I arrive.

The camels appear like dark, formless shapes at first because my mind is still in a state of disbelief. I see the pen and the storehouse and the bed. I've come in from the side. It seems I have been stalking the sides of the pasture the whole time. I'm in the middle of nowhere, yet I feel like I'm lying down in the cosy living room with my family in Jeddah. I run. Relief pours down my skin. I need water. Fast.

The creatures despised have now saved my life. Camels are the lions of the desert. Abram turns from the pen and sees me. I nod to him. He gives me a half-smile, like he knows I got lost but is pretending not to notice the panic frozen on my face. He hands me a bottle of water, then turns back to the pen.

I never told Abram that I was lost or that it was the tracks that saved me. But this evening, I spend a long time thinking about the uncertainty I felt and the moment of simple surrender when I was most in despair.

I am having mixed feelings towards camels. How can I despise an animal that did not hurt me, yet saved my life in a way? How can I accept good deeds from someone I only imagine negative? I was never harmed by them, yet I perceive that what I feel for them is only dislike.

Night falls very softly here, and then it inks very dark, unlike in the city where we poke the night sky with city lights to keep it from blackening. Once the sheep settle down, I lie down on my bed and remember today. I was lost, physically. But I was always lost before that, mentally. I did not know it until the moment of failure out in the desert hit me and reminded me to think. Becoming lost was a physical failure, and when I threw a rock at the sheep, that was the mental failure. My heart was not beating hard when I failed then: my ego was hurt.

Now that I am safe on my bed, I think that getting lost might have been a good thing. I realise now that I lost my sense of myself too when I failed: I need to find myself and get back on track.

I fall back on my bed like a dead man and drop quickly into sleep, in supreme gratitude that I am simply alive and here. I may not have found the epiphany that I was after yet, but for this moment of complete bliss, it has all been worth it so far.

Jeddah, Saudi Arabia, 2013

As I work through the school term, some problems begin to arise, as they would in any organisation. I set out to solve each one according to the school's operational plan, which I conjured into being because it did not have one to begin with. The managerial and technical problems that come my way are easy to solve, but downright disregard of my leadership is not.

The head of the middle-school division clearly has doubts about whether or not a twenty-nine-year-old can run the school. He never does any of the things I ask him to do to follow our operational plan. He avoids me in the hallways and rarely answers my calls.

So I decide a surprise visit to his office might be a good idea. When I arrive, I find he is in a meeting with some middle-school teachers. My polite inclination is to wait until his meeting is over, but something in me makes me act.

I knock on his door and go in. I quietly observe the teachers sitting on chairs in a half-circle. They quietly observe me back. Before it turns into a stare-down, I ask them to give us the room.

'I need to speak to Ustaz F. T. in privacy,' I say.

The gentlemen leave the room. Ustaz F. T. remains at his desk, looking like he's gathering all his resources to fend off any form of authority coming from me. I close the door and sit down.

'Ustaz F. T., I have decided to be direct with you,' I begin. 'I'm only going to ask you one question.'

He waits. I can see a glimmer of curiosity fighting through his defences.

'Does it bother you that I was once your student?'

His face falls. His defences come crashing down.

'No!' he says. 'Of course not!'

I know it does, or at least I believe that.

'It makes me proud to see one of my own students succeed and rise up to such a position.'

Now this is a man who I know loves prestige and 'positions'. I nod in confirmation. I try to speak his language of communication, and be genuine in what I will say.

'I truly appreciate you saying that. We cannot become who we are without our education and the people who helped us grow. And you were one of them.'

His face breaks into an irrevocable smile. He's won.

9

Trust: the truth will set you free

In the end, it's not going to matter how many breaths you took, but how many moments took your breath away.

Shing Xiong

The Nufuth Desert, 2011: Day Seven

On the seventh day I wake up to do my chores. I realise there is a lot of pent-up energy in my body that must have accumulated during the night. I'm sensitive to the air by now. I can sense that the weather will be a few degrees cooler today than it was yesterday.

Abram has not arrived yet. I feel like the desert knows me by now. It's not the gentlest teacher. It's not the most hospitable host. But it knows me and acknowledges me as one of its own. I rather like that, so I greet it with a grin. I bounce from place to place, feeling my muscles hum pleasantly as I lift the bales of hay and grass and throw them into the pen. Without bothering to open the gate, simply because I'm enjoying the activity, I lift myself and jump over the fence. I fill the water tank. I cut the rope that ties the bales of hay together and set it loose on the ground. And then something happens like a single resonating tone that you cannot miss.

Something nuzzles me from behind. A lamb has come to me.

I am struck with sudden fondness. One of them has finally approached, and it is the youngest. I kneel slowly onto the ground, afraid to scare it away. I pick up a reed of grass and present it to the lamb.

It smells the grass, it smells my hand, and then quickly snatches the grass and bends to munch on it. Maybe I'm not an animal whisperer. If I were, this lamb would have been cuddling on my lap a long time ago. But in the past six difficult days, I have transformed into the apprentice of an animal whisperer, or a believer in animal whispering.

The lamb trots away when its mother approaches tentatively to protect it. I believe I may have used up my luck for the day. I get up and lift the bales so I can place them in the centre of the pen like I always do.

I carry the piles of grass and hay. The sheep scatter away. I place the food in the centre and busy myself spreading it into four even piles so that they can share fairly. As I'm absorbed in doing this, I feel heat and smell a rank odour near my right shoulder. One of the adult sheep has come close to watch. I look up in astonishment.

The others follow suit. Slowly, the entire herd has gathered around me and is now feeding, with me in the centre. I am too afraid to move. Too afraid to jump, or whoop, or scream, or laugh. My six days in this forlorn place have now solidified into one moment: the moment I sit in the centre of a feeding herd, unable to move because I am too thankful that they have simply accepted my presence. I am valid in their existence. I am a human they know. I am AlBaraa, not quite a shepherd, but I'm the sheep's casual friend who they call up on Fridays to watch the game. That is enough for me.

Things are coming to a close. It's midday and I'm feeling anxious. It's like someone came and turned off the projector before the movie ended. I want to go home now.

I feel there is nothing left for me to learn because I am awash with a sense of completion. I know that the next three days, if I stay, will not make me more of a shepherd. The epiphany I was waiting for arrived this morning.

The joy of my success rings true and solid, even now, hours later. Perseverance. Trust. Gradual acceptance. I've taken the lead by leading myself, every single day, to prove to these gentle creatures that I am their friend. Finally, I am one of their own as I huddle there in the middle of their piles of food. I have broken through.

It really all starts with trust, and you know that you are trusted by proximity. With the animals, the proximity is physical. They trust you enough to approach you. With humans, the proximity is emotional, when they come to you with their problems, gossip and day-to-day issues. They come to you for advice, support, solutions – even action. Trust is the jewel I was after. I needed to see it happening and unfolding before my eyes. You need trust to build a foundation for good leadership, but I've realised I'm not after leadership in the general sense. I'm after that authentic brand of leadership that stems from caring, and I believe this is what all Koranic and biblical prophets were able to master, which shepherding helped them learn. They led and guided nations to salvation because they appealed to the people's trust. *But what comes before trust?* I ask myself, now that it's all becoming clear. Caring. And showing up every single time you're needed. Trust increases in a continuum of connecting and caring. The more we connect, the more we understand, and the more we understand, the more our care becomes personalised and meaningful. The continuum is unending, with loops of learning and feedback. With every round, I failed, but it is only because I accepted failure and was eager to learn that I managed to offer care again. As we learn more, our failures are greater, and if we offer care in its many forms, we will learn more, and fail more. Trust will only come from the commitment to care and learn, continuously.

I really feel like leaving now. Staying here even one more day does not make sense. I want to fly back to Boston with what I've learned. I'm excited to leave! Plus, I need to talk to someone. I desperately want to talk to my family. A phone call right now with my mother or grandmother would be the grand prize of this experience. It astonishes me to realise that feeling alone around people is much more bearable than having no option but loneliness. Then it occurs to me this is probably exactly how Abram feels out here.

I am ecstatic and thankful. So deeply thankful.

10

The Shepherd Leader for the modern world

I left the desert with a hunger to share my experience with people, to exchange ideas, to communicate with another human being about all the hardship I went through in just a week. Keeping my abnormal thoughts to myself was difficult. At this point, you have the choice to continue reading my takeaways from the experience and what I have learned, or to leave with yours.

After shepherding, I had four opportunities to experience the concepts of Shepherd Leadership. As a fresh graduate from the desert, I worked at DAT school and managed to apply all the concepts I had learned in the desert. The results were extraordinary. As much as numbers are important in showing progress, I would like to share two stories that speak beyond numbers, and concern people's emotions and behaviours. After all, 'The Modern Shepherd' is a people-centric strategy for a new leadership style, a value-based leadership.

As I was doing my routine round, talking to the staff in the main administration hall of the school, one of the parents arrived, wanting to register his fourth-year son. The administration hall is a large square with offices at its corners, an exhibition on one side showing the achievements and values of the school, and the entrance to the academic area of the school. I welcomed the father and walked him to the registration office to sign up his son for next year, but the registrar was out of the office at that time. So, I asked him if he wanted to take a tour of the school, and I would tell him all about what we are doing, our academic programmes, extracurricular activities, sport and entertainment facilities, tell him our plans to improve the school, and answer all of his questions. He shook my hand and told me his name, and I responded with mine.

'You are AlBaraa Taibah?'

I confirmed yes.

'You are the one working in this school development?'

I said that I was one of the team members who were doing that, yes. What he said next puts me in tears every time I remember this story.

'I am transferring my son to this school because of you.'

I ran out of words, and all my energy flew to my heart with gratitude and happiness. 'Thank you, I really appreciate that. Shall we?'

In the desert, I worked on my care, and my grit to earn the trust of the people I cared about. In the school, trust was transferred beyond the people to whom I directly offered care. It was surprising to learn that trust is infectious by reputation and word of mouth. What greater show of trust can there be than putting your own son in the hands of someone else? I am grateful, and eternally proud of this moment.

A few months after this incident, I was head-hunted to lead the National Programme for Teacher Standards and Licensing in Saudi Arabia.

The programme aimed to raise the quality of over five hundred thousand teachers in Saudi. When I decided to accept the offer, I announced to everyone in the school that, by the end of the first semester of the school year 2014–15, I would move to another challenge. My feelings were mixed as I wanted to support the kids of this one school, but I also had the chance to have an impact on every teacher in Saudi, including those in this school. I was hesitant to accept the offer, as I wanted more experience on the ground before leading a national project in education, but then a dear friend told me a quote by Richard Branson: 'Fly and find your wings on the way down.' So I did.

A few days later, one of the top-performing teachers in the school came to my office to extend his condolences that I was leaving. After we talked for a while about the new job, he asked, 'Who will solve our issues, Mr AlBaraa, after you leave?'

'But you have never come to me about any issues before!' I responded with surprise. What he said afterwards touched me, as it related to one of the major goals I wanted to achieve, the one that Ms Ellen had taught me about education leadership.

'True, I did not come to you with an issue. But everyone in the school is comfortable in the knowledge that if he has an issue, you will solve it.'

It is not only trust that is contagious, but care is too! I believe that behavioural styles are a leader's brand and identity. Behaviours are the basis of leadership, skills come next. As we grow in our careers, our actions and behaviours move with us. The Shepherd Leadership brand is a people-centric brand: to connect and care, to fail and learn, and to commit and trust. Leading against people will be a failed endeavour. Lead with them, grow with them, and celebrate with them.

Not all my attempts to experience the Shepherd Leadership style were successful. I failed because I deprioritised connections and relationships in favour of deliverables when I was leading the project for the development of a national strategy. I delivered, but then failed in the long run. I accepted the learning opportunity, but I did not accept that I was not connecting enough at the time, and still could not prioritise people over deliverables. All the reasons why I did what I did can be categorised as excuses, and I learned a lot from that team.

I am no shepherd, and I don't own a staff. I lived for one week in the desert to understand why all prophets shepherded at some point in their life. I knew there was a relationship between shepherding and leadership, but I did not know what. The books did not fulfil my recurring questions. I was seeking to understand leadership from a unique and different perspective. The 'Ten-Steps-to-Become-a-Leader' books did not touch upon the practicality I sought; I sought answers to my questions about how to lead in reality rather than 'what is leadership?'. I wanted to learn by doing, not in classrooms. Many can learn in classrooms but, if I get to choose, I prefer experience.

Shepherd Leadership is a value-based approach to leadership emphasising how leaders should place people first. It is practical, effective and broad enough that leaders can utilise the traits that exist in their everyday lives. It is speaking about the software of leadership, not the hardware of actions and activities. Values and human interactions are the foundation of every relationship; skills and competencies follow. Both are important, but leaders will not make getting the first element right.

The Shepherd Leadership concept is needed today, as technology is bringing us closer but our emotional state is pushed further into the background. According to Six Seconds' 'State of the

Heart' report in 2016, 'around the globe, emotional intelligence has been on the decline since 2011'. We are living in a different time: the twenty-first century brought the fourth industrial revolution with it, with smart technology changing manufacturing, communication and the way we live and work. As corporations and governments push for technological and economic progress, today's leaders will need to pursue the concepts of Shepherd Leadership. Almost all of us are impacted by technological development and how this is altering the fabric of society both professionally and personally. I remember family dinners with no phones back in the 1990s, and friendships consisting of quality time together rather than reading a status update. Leaders of today, more than ever, need to prioritise values and human connections.

In Shepherd Leadership, it all starts with expectations. Equipping your skills and mind to what is coming next, understanding the expectations of others, and setting the right expectations for the path ahead. Unlike the flock of sheep, people have expectations and they will judge accordingly. Furthermore, setting the leader's expectations is just as important. Many warned me about the desert, but only Abu Bandar set the bar high enough when he said 'Beware of death.' Everything that happened to me was manageable, as it was below my expectations.

Even if we equip ourselves with the right mindset and the perfect state of the heart, we all pass through difficulties and challenges. We get lost, we fail and we get rejected, in my case by animals. Will is the first part of the Level 5 Leadership equation in Jim Collins's *Good to Great*. Challenges are small quizzes and tests to prove that we are worthy of facing what is coming up next in our path. No celebrity, entrepreneur or self-made millionaire will tell you it was easy, and none will say they made it with without facing any challenges. They all had doubts at one point, and thought that they should stop, or were not capable, or could not make it. Yet, they energised their souls with the will to continue and proved to themselves that they are worthy, one challenge at a time.

Setting expectations and having willpower means focusing on oneself. The first step in leading others is to connect, with the empathy to understand the other side's pains, fears, hopes and needs. Connect to understand how you could show that you care, even with a small gesture such as a pat on the back at the right time. The flock did not care that my new title was 'shepherd', or probably 'intern shepherd'. They did not respond positively to my efforts to connect. People will react the same: they will not open up because a CEO asked, or a general manager proactively tried to connect. Actions are the key to their hearts.

Connecting is a two-way path: connect with yourself first, then connect with others. As a leader, understanding your strengths for better utilisation and admitting your weaknesses while being humble and open to learning will open the connections with others. We cannot offer what we do not have, and if we don't care enough about ourselves, caring about others will not be sustainable.

Care is at the core of the Shepherd Leader. Taking care to understand, care to support and care to connect. The continuation of caring and connecting will result in an increase of relationship trust. The more you connect, the more you understand how you can care better, and the more you can offer the right care at the right time.

Do not be afraid of learning, and that is what I call failing. Learn from your failure and try not to fail twice at the same thing. The education system does not understand failure. We tell students that perfection is the best grade you can get, but nothing in real life is perfect. We celebrate a student with an A grade, and we do not go back to teach them what they did wrong, so that they can still learn. We push for book smart and not practice smart. We push for memorisation and not understanding. We punish students who have talents we did not discover; a student with a D in maths, a student with a different answer, a student with no interest in science topics, an introverted student who does not participate in class, and many more. Mistakes are fun. Failure is learning. A teacher with no-mistakes-students should be replaced with another realistic teacher! Failure is important in schools, where there is no real-life accountability. Failure is important at work, where there is accountability. Learning through failure is the path towards growth. Humans are the only creatures on Planet Earth that can expand the possibilities of learning and grow as a result, so let's make use of this unique feature.

The continuation of connecting to care and caring to connect will result in a trusting relationship. Learning expedites achieving that trusting relationship. Reaching a trusting relationship will open all doors to apply your technical knowledge and skills. Of course, you do not have to wait for full trust to activate this: it is a balanced relationship. Finally, make use of that work you have done to promote care and trust as a brand; the stronger the brand, the more stakeholders it will reach.

Today in 2019, I still think back to nine years ago to remember the first time I decided to shepherd. I wanted to know why all prophets used to shepherd at some point in their lives. I wanted to understand what these individuals learned, what enabled them to win the hearts of the billions who have followed them for centuries, and relate that to leaders in the modern world. I wanted to learn leadership differently, to witness it in practice.

I expected my experience in the desert to answer the question why all prophets shepherded. I was ready to learn, but never thought that the dumb flock and the super-hot desert would completely change my perspective of leadership. I am grateful, and consider this experience a pivotal point in my leadership practices. I am taking this knowledge, similar to you now, and trying to apply the Shepherd Leader concepts in my professional life. I am still learning, continuously growing, and hope you are too.